MARTHA'S GOT NOTHIN' ON ME

The PRE-FAB
Cookbook
by DISH & FLO

For the Cooking-Impaired and Gourmet Alike

Characters are copyrights and trademarks of Left Field Productions.
Published by Winding Stair Press.

In U.S. —
Winding Stair Press
1180 Medical Court, Suite A,
Carmel, Indiana
40632
and in Canada —
Winding Stair Press
290 North Queen St., Suite 210
Etobicoke, Ontario
M9C 5K4

National Library of Canada Cataloguing in Publication Data

Bishop, Debbie
       Martha s got nothin on me : the pre-fab cookbook
Includes index.

ISBN 1-55366-157-5
    1. Quick and easy cookery. I. Berg, Cori II. Title.

TX833.5.B57 2001   641.5'55   C2001-903281-1

1 2 3 4 5 6

Publisher: Ken Proctor
Publishing Director: Joe March
Written by: Debbie Bishop & Cori Berg
Illustrations by: Rick Tierney & Debbie Bishop
Book Design by: Debbie Bishop
Edited by: Cori Berg & Barbara Palermo
Printed and bound in Canada

This book is available at special discounts for bulk purchases by groups or organizations for sales promotions, premiums, fund-raising, & educational purposes.

For details contact:
Winding Stair Press
Special Sales Department
1-866-574-6873

Microwave Cooking: Microwave ovens vary in wattage. The cooking times suggested in this book are approximate. Use them as guidelines and check for doneness before adding more time or consuming the food. Consult your microwave manufacturer s guidelines for suitable microwave-safe cooking dishes.

This book is dedicated to
the guy or gal with the six kids
(or one two-year-old),
the stressful job with long hours,
the demanding partner
or, *God help you honey* ~
all of the above!

We believe, there are two things we must do in life:

Enjoy it
&
Get your hair done once in awhile.

Nothing gives me greater pleasure than being able to spend all day watching old Doris Day movies by the fire while cooking a cozy four-course meal for the family from scratch. The kids make crafts and the hubby shouts instructions to the boys playing sports on TV. Ahh, pure heaven. However, I only had one day last year where I was able to find the time to do that. These days, it seems, even finding time to make holiday cookies is difficult. What's a gal to do?

Fake it, honey. You know, for years I thought my brother made the best seafood gumbo I've ever tasted. I asked him for the recipe recently, and you know what he said? "Go down to the chicken place on the corner and pick up a quart." And I thought I invented "Pre-Fab."

The word comes from those pre-fabricated houses...you know, the ones that are built in a factory, trucked to a lot and put up in a few days. They're usually more affordable than building one individual home because the manufacturers' costs are spread out over several houses. The buyers snazz them up with paint and landscaping and make them their own. I thought if they can make homes that way, we should be able to do the same with food.

Why should we spend all our free time cooking? There are so many fabulous pre-fab foods to choose from. We can pick something up from the grocer and doll it up a bit ~nobody needs to know we didn't make it from scratch.

I've found that I save money this way, too. I don't know about you, but unless I label leftovers with signs that say "It's okay to eat this until such-and-such a day...REALLY!", they don't get eaten. Even with labels, they don't always get eaten. With pre-fab foods, there is usually less waste, because I can buy in quantities just large enough for the meal. And I don't have to get all of those other ingredients that I might not use.

Flo's an exception. She really makes her meals. She's a wonderful gourmet cook of those delicious old-fashioned foods that we all grew up with. When I showed her my original book, she said, "You know, you really ought to put some recipes in it."

So there you have it, the story of how our cookbook came to be. A combination of quick and easy or ready made dishes and recipes that might take awhile. There are fat-free and fat-full ideas. (*No guilt allowed.*) You can decide how much effort to put into your meals. But, honey, don't work too hard~we all deserve a little pampering now and then.

Dish & Flo

Table of Contents

PRE-FAB IT!

Pre-Fab it

Who has time to cook anymore?

Pick up pre-made foods and snazz them up when you get home. Presentation is the key. No one needs to know that you didn't slave all day in the kitchen. Your grocer has everything you need to cook the pre-fab way. Use the time you save on you!

Deli-counter

It's cheaper to buy what you want, pre-made, than buying all the ingredients separately and spending the time making it~it's a lot easier, too. Especially if you're serving just a few friends. Pre-Fab foods from the deli counter save loads of time and money, not too mention ~ your manicure. Be sure to taste them first, though. Most delis will gladly give you a small taste of something. Unfortunately, most will eventually catch on to "grazing ."
You know...trying all the different samples until you're stuffed, grabbing your stomach, letting out a great big "AAAHHHH that was good" and walking away without buying a thing!

Salad Bar

Most grocery stores have a salad bar these days. It's so handy.
When you're out of time or cooking for just a few, buy your veggies already cut up. (Tasting here is a no-no. Take my word for it and save yourself the embarrassment of being scolded by a grocery store manager with the deepest blue eyes you've ever seen!) On second thought...

Refrigerated Pasta Section

Fabulous packaged sauces and fresh pastas. Try a new sauce with your favorite fresh noodle. Doll it up by adding more vegetables, clams or shrimp. Serve with grated Parmesan and Romano cheeses. Top with fresh chopped basil. *Garlic lovers ~ sprinkle in an extra bit. If you serve it to everybody, no one will notice how bad you smell.*

Bakery

No need to bake ~ buy it already done! Order what you need ahead of time
or take what they have and jazz it up when you get home.
For that fresh-baked smell, see the *Kitchen Secrets* section of this book.

Fruit Salad

Forget chopping all that fruit. The store has marvelous fruit salads already cut up! You can
even get fruit salad made to order! Call the deli! Choose your fruit, serve it in a pretty bowl
and garnish with fresh berries or a mint leaf ~ Or ~ have them make it in a watermelon
basket. When your friends compliment you on your beautiful buffet, just say "Thank you!"

Garlic

Why get it all over your hands?
I buy mine by the jar. Crushed garlic packed in it's own juice (without oil). Check out the
produce section. Fresh ginger is also a wonderful flavor enhancer to keep in stock.

Have It Delivered!

Best time saver of all. You can touch up your "do" while you wait for dinner.
Order ahead and nuke it (microwave) before your guests arrive.

IT'S ALL IN THE AMBIANCE

IT'S ALL IN THE AMBIANCE

Presentation is what makes eating fun.
It also makes the food look better.
Whenever I really screw up a meal, we eat by candlelight.

THEMES

Every holiday has a color. Use it in your meals and accessories.
Be creative! Add some of your personal pizzaz to every occasion.

NEW YEAR'S DAY

Anything goes! With the way you probably feel after last night's party -
Forget cooking. Scrounge the kitchen for nukeable food .

Bright Idea - Prepare your New Year's Day feast before your New Year's Eve party --
when you're not hung-over.

VALENTINE'S DAY

One rose, a red teddy and finger food.
Got kids?
Feed them turkey. It will make them sleepy and you guys can get back to the finger food.

ST. PATRICK'S DAY

Everything green. Green Dip. Green napkins. Green Marganita.
Place a four-leaf clover on your lover's pillow and tell them it's their lucky day!

EASTER

Go pastel.   Serve everything in baskets lined with colorful napkins.
Arrange Easter grass and jelly beans on your buffet table.
Do your hunt differently this year - put the eggs out and hide the kids.

MOTHER'S DAY
Go out.

MEMORIAL DAY

Have a blast. Invite the gang over. Bright colors. Big earrings.
Serve zombies and barbeque shishkabobs by the pool.
No pool? Try one of those blow-up jobs to liven your bash.

The next day, walk wide-eyed up to your best friend and ask if she remembers what she
did at the party. Then say, "You don't?" Laugh and walk away.

FATHER'S DAY

Anything goes with sports. It's funny - men will eat almost anything in front of the television.
Don't spend a lot of time preparing it - they won't notice unless it's wearing a remote control.
Hey, you might try that idea on the hubby.

INDEPENDENCE DAY

Red, white and blue fruit salad over pound cake with whipped cream.
Or break out that red teddy, garnish yourself with blueberries and whipped cream
and let the sparks fly!

SUMMER LUAU

Cut out paper fish - have the kids color them while you and your significant other
practice the hula - if you know what I mean.

LABOR DAY

Let someone else cook. Go out for a massage.

FIRST DAY OF AUTUMN

Good excuse to wear orange. Decorate your table with some fallen leaves from your yard.
Replace your regular light bulbs with yellow ones for a little cozy ambiance!

HALLOWEEN

Be bad! Throw a no-costume party but "forget" to tell that back-stabber "friend"
of yours not to dress up.

Make black frosted cupcakes with pipe-cleaner legs and gummy candy eyes.
Decorate with fake spider webs and dramatic lighting. Play spooky audio tapes and music.

Make your "friend" feel better by letting her answer the door and give candy to
all the trick-or-treaters - then you can get back to your party.

I usually just go without makeup on Halloween and scare the heck out of everybody!

Go Veggie!

THANKSGIVING

Relax this year. Order everything prepared from your grocer or deli.
Have your guests bring a dish (most people like to contribute something to the dinner).
Buy a few pumpkins and mums to put around the house and go do your nails.
Enjoy the party for a change.

HANUKKAH

Go to his mother's. Give her the joy of cooking for the whole family, eight days in a row.

CHRISTMAS

One Christmas morning, in a strange city, everything was closed.
We found a forlorn little Christmas tree by the side of the road and took it to our motel.
It didn't have a stand, so we hung it from the ceiling with fishing line.
It made me realize, that it doesn't matter how much or how little you have on this day,
the important thing is spending it with people you care about
~ And it helps to have nice neighbors with food.

Wait! Who am I kidding? Pull out all the stops!
Decorate everything that isn't nailed down with bows, fresh greenery, pine cones and lights.
Set a table with enough food for the last supper (pre-fab of course!)
Buy all those cute little candies and pastries for your dessert table.
Decorate your plate rack with fresh cedar and ribbons.
Wear your battery-packed apron with the blinking Christmas lights. Serve spiced cider
from your crock pot while humming Christmas carols.   Add extra rum
to the egg nog and meet that someone special under the mistletoe...What's that?
The line forms to the left? Goose? No, I don't want a Christmas goose! Hey, watch it!

 # NEW YEAR'S EVE
Family Fun

Throw a slumber party! Dance and play games all night. Decorate with balloons, streamers
and confetti. Make lots of buffet-style foods - Sandwich fixin's, crab or spinach dip,
fresh vegetable and fruit trays. Better yet, order a pizza or submarine sandwich.
At midnight, bang pots and pans together as noisemakers (or wake up the kids).

The next morning watch the parades on TV. You can use some of your leftovers to make
scrambled eggs. Serve them with muffins and jam by the television.

 ## Ritzy New Year's Eve
Make it a black-tie affair.
Cover the ceiling with helium-filled balloons tied with ribbons. Curl the ends with a dull
knife. Use metallic or colorful streamers and confetti all over the house. Order from a
gourmet grocery store and serve buffet-style using your best crystal and glass dinnerware.
Offer finger sandwiches, caviar loaf, mousse pate´, smoked salmon, varieties of crackers,
melon balls, champagne or sparkling cider. Turn the lights down and play music from
your favorite decade.

Easy Entertaining Tips
How much time do you have?

Lots of Time

PICK YOUR THEME
Choose your colors. Carry them through, from flowers and linens to guest soaps and toilet paper. The day of the party, wear clothes that compliment your colors and don't clash.

CASUAL OR FORMAL
Baskets and bowls vs. crystal and silver.
Sometimes it's fun to go nutty. Use tacky, bright colored plastic to serve your food in.
Decorate 60's space-age style, like in the cartoons.
Wear your hair like the Big Dipper with a huge flip on one side.
(Tip ~Don't turn your head too fast, you might knock someone over.)

BUFFET OR SIT-DOWN
Buffet style ~ big flowers. Sit-down dinners ~ low flower arrangements
~ unless of course, you've invited someone you don't really want to see.

FLOWERS
Have 'em delivered! Or mix and match bouquets from the grocery store.
Tip: Cut the ends off under water, they'll last longer. Adding a bit of crushed aspirin,
vitamin C or sugar to the water will make your flowers last longer as well.
Unless you're a whiz at flower arranging and enjoy doing it, don't spend a lot of time.
In most cases, less is more ~ and usually is better for the budget.
A few glads in a vase are quite lovely.

BASKET STYLE

Serve your food in baskets lined with linen napkins.
Surround a bowl of dip with veggies or chips. Arrange fresh fruit and/or vegetables in baskets.
They're not only attractive, they're delicious! *(The fruit...not the baskets.)*

For fruit, scoop out the center of a melon to serve dip in. For vegetables, use the center of red
cabbage or a bell pepper for your dip. Serve your other dry foods in baskets, too.
Easy clean up! Save the bowls and platters for the wet stuff.

Linen napkins make
wonderful liners
for serving in baskets!

TABLE MOTIF

Go feminine.
Throw a solid-colored tablecloth over your table. Cover it with a lace one (or another tablecloth
of a different color). Gather the ends of the top tablecloth and tie them with a ribbon.
Tuck flowers into each bow. Add English ivy, jasmine or pine to the bows.
Tie up, uh, tie in your theme!

MORE TABLE MOTIF

For a child's party, slip toy characters into the tied ends of your tablecloth.
Decorate your food with toy figurines that your child's friends can take home.

Throw a mystery party!
Choose your mystery from a game or create of your own. Hide clues inside the dinner napkins
and around the table. Solve the mystery during dinner! Keep the answer handy, though. When
all of the eyes at the table turn and look at you for the answer,
it's a good idea to know what it is.

Or ~ Not only are you out of time, but someone forgot to run the dishwasher!

PURPOSELY   SCATTERED

Serve buffet style.
Use whatever's clean ~ Different types of bowls and baskets lined with napkins.
Place Gerbera daisies in cups and position them in several places on your table.
Mix up the colors. Alternate your plate patterns. Wear two different earrings and colorful clothes.
Serve two kinds of dip. Tell 'em it's a "California thing ." No one will ever know!

DISASTER ZONE

The babysitter let the kids run wild, the house is a mess
and company is coming in twenty minutes! What do you do? Well ~
Throw the toys in the closet, get the living, dining and guest bathroom in order.
Toss your take-out food in some nice bowls and arrange the table.
Place candles in safe areas and light them.
Now, go outside and turn the electricity off at the fuse box.
Tell your guests you had a power outage. (*But look! I was able to save dinner!*)

Set the kids up with flashlights and coloring books.
They'll have a ball pretending they're camping. No one will see your messy house.

P.S. -- Fire the babysitter.

Pizzaz

COLORED LIGHTS

Light bulbs are fun to decorate with. Color changes the entire feel of a room. Yellow bulbs give it a warm, cozy feeling. Red adds drama. Pink makes us all look prettier by giving us the illusion of a healthy glow. Green and blue are hard to see by, but can be fun if you don't have a lot of furniture to trip over.

CULTURE FUN

It's also fun "Cooking with Cultures ." You can make a meal that's popular in a certain country, then decorate your table with colors and flowers from that country. Check out the encyclopedia or contact a library through the Internet for info on the country or culture of your choice. Or — just wing it. Your guests will most likely enjoy anything you try.
Make up a culture of your own.

Like the land of Schnarfwitz ~ where you serve extra napkins because people are always sneezing at the odor from the cheese factory. It's where the saying "Who cut the cheese?" originated.
Of course it had an entirely different meaning in Schnarfwitz.

PARTY BUFFETS

Buffet style is about the only way I do parties anymore. The food goes in one place. Less decorating, less clean-up. Plus, I think people like being able to pick out the foods they want without the pressure of thinking they have to eat everything.
Tip ~ If you're really hungry...strike up a conversation with someone right next to the buffet table. You can scarf down your food and get seconds without anyone *really* noticing.

BASKETS

Baskets are great to serve in! Line them with colorful linens. After the party, all you have to do is shake out the linens and throw them in the washer! No dishes to wash.
Of course, they're not real good for serving fondue.

CAUTION WITH CANDLES

I've learned not to use candles on a buffet. I'm usually the klutz that almost knocks them over.
And then there's the little matter of fire insurance.
They told me if I used candles they'd have to increase my premiums.
With the amount of hair spray in my *"do"*, they say I'm a fire hazard.

CHEAP DECOR

Decorating the buffet or dinner table doesn't have to cost a bundle. You'd be surprised at what
you can find in your garden. Small ivy or jasmine is wonderful wound around a plate rack.
Little pine branches, juniper and pine cones make a fabu winter display.
Whole vegetables arranged in a basket look great on a table. And, of course, flowers are nice too.
Shake the spiders out, though, especially from garden roses.
Nothing says "stale food" more than spider webs.

Be careful not to use flowers that may be poisonous around the food.
You don't really want to knock off Aunt Mabel.

Check with your local poison control center if you know the names of the plants you'd like to
use. Oleander and poinsettias are poisonous. Pansies and Violas are not, unless they've been
exposed to pesticides. If you're not sure, arrange the plants and flowers in places where they
won't touch or fall into the food. Or use plastic! Tell your friends you're re-living the 60's!
Whatever you do though - leave those hip-hugger bellbottoms in the closet!
Some things don't deserve to be reborn.

KIDS' PARTY IDEAS

PICK YOUR THEME

Choose party plates and decorations to match your theme.
Have your baker match the cake or cupcakes to your theme.

CUT UP FOOD

Kids love finger foods.   Use cookie cutters to cut sandwiches and quesadillas into shapes. Or cut them into quarters, triangle or squares.   Serve cheese and crackers. Skewer raisins, bananas and apple chunks on toothpicks (for older kids). Tie food bundles with licorice ropes.

GUMMY BOWLS

Gummies are a must. They come in all sorts of shapes and sizes to use as garnishes for your recipes. Pour some in a bowl for the kids to munch on.

CREEPY MUD PIE

Chocolate pudding over a crushed cookie crust, gummy candy worms and bugs squished into the pudding. Top with whipped cream. Sprinkle more cookie crumbs on the sides and top for "dirt ." Make one big pie or individual servings in paper cups.

FLAVORED GELATIN

Flavored Gelatin is great for any party -- First, pick your gummies, then prepare an appropriate color gelatin. Add the gummies when cool, just before gelatin sets.

Blue - Toss in some shark and fish gummies before the gelatin sets. Shape waves out of whipped topping, use crushed cookies for sand and
top with a couple of action heroes, fishing, just for laughs.

Green - Almost any gummy shape will do - bugs, flowers, etc.

Yellow - Fruit-shaped gummies.

Halloween - Orange or purple gelatin with black bats, spiders or white ghost gummies.

Quesadillas

Flour or corn tortillas
Grated cheese

Individual - Sprinkle grated cheese on a tortilla. Place in microwave. Nuke for about 1 minute until the cheese melts. Remove and fold in half or roll.

Place the hot tortillas in a baking dish side by side like little tacos. Fill each one with grated cheese and roll them up. Microwave for about 1 minute until the cheese is fully melted. Cut into 1-inch pieces or fun shapes. Arrange on a platter. Serve warm.

For a party - pre-heat the tortillas in the microwave between 2 paper towels for about 30 seconds to 60 seconds on high. The cheese should melt faster this way.

Quick & Easy Marshmallow Crisp Treats

3 Tbsp. butter
4 cups mini-marshmallows
6 cups rice cereal

Now, before the kids get home, don't let those buttered hands go to waste! Try them out on someone you love.

Melt butter and marshmallows in microwave 2 min. Stir, then nuke 1 more minute. Add the rice cereal and stir. Spray a 13 x 9-inch pan with low-fat cooking spray. Spread mixture into pan using buttered hands or buttered wax paper. Cool, cut and decorate. Use candy corn, jelly beans, raisins, red hots, tie like a package with licorice ropes.

Peppermint Orange

Oranges
Straight peppermint candy canes

Place your palm on the orange and gently roll around on the counter to loosen the juices. Cut a small hole in the orange. Insert a candy cane.

Suck on the candy cane like a straw to get the juice from the orange.

24

TEEN PARTY IDEAS
Set disposable cameras around and let them go for it!

FOOD
Keep it simple. Pizza - pepperoni and cheese. Submarine sandwiches, microwave popcorn, soda or instant cappuccino. Bowl of candy bars.

PRETEEN BOYS & GIRLS
Let them bake something. Buy prepared cookie dough, set up everything for sugar cookie decorating - canned frosting, decorative icing tubes, candy toppings. (See the cake decorating section of your store).   They can eat or take home their creations. Food fights *may* happen. Be prepared, wrap the kids in hefty bags with holes cut out for their head and arms.

GIRLS
Cell phones, fashion and gossip magazines, hunk videos (PG), and good music. Keep them busy doing makeup, nails, hair, or some easy crafts. Ask for suggestions at your local craft store. Take them on a scavenger hunt (to safe places and people you know).

BOYS
Action videos, computer and video games. Let them make model cars or paper airplanes. Keep tape, pennies and paperclips on hand for airplane repairs. Have contests for distance, height, best design, best modified, etc. Outdoor activities - Take them to the movies, roller-hockey rink, batting cages or miniature golf.

FUN PARTY LOCATIONS
Local park, beach, backyard, pizza parlor, amusement park, water park, burger joint, mall food court, video game arcade, slot car raceway or local 50's diner (bring lots of quarters for the juke box).

GAL PARTIES

Invite the girls over for a slumber party. Give yourselves manicures, facials and hair treatments. Nibble on healthful snacks, pig out on junk food or both!

Stock up on current fashion and gossip magazines. Set up tables with bowls of "bod" treatments and manicure sets. *(Manicure set: clippers, emery boards, orange sticks, cuticle cream, polish remover, cotton, nail polish)*.   Tell the gals to bring their own make-up mirror *(so you can all do yourselves at the same time.)* Have a few extras around though, in case somebody forgets.
Lay towels, wash cloths and a nail scrubber next to the sink.
Set up hair treatments, shampoo, conditioner, brushes, combs, curlers, blow dryer, curling iron, mousse and hair spray for finishing touches.

After treatments, pass around a basket of scented lotions to complete your body beautiful session. Relax and gossip over instant cappuccinos *(don't forget to make the coffee machine noise)*, topped with whipped cream and sprinkles. Fresh fruit parfaits with nonfat frozen yogurt or brownies and ice cream smothered in Kahlua or Bailey's Irish Creme will finish you off.

STUD NIGHT

The guys are coming over to play some cards? Alright. Set the card table up near the TV so you can watch the game while you're playing. Set up the video and computer games, too.
You can play them during commercials when that friend of yours who always takes too long is deciding which card to throw down.

Food - Pretzels, beer, submarine sandwiches, pizza, chips, dip, cookies ~ that kind of junk.

Ha! 4 Aces!
That means you
have to be the
bearing wall, Bill!"

ACCESSORIZE

ACCESSORIZE

Snazz up those dishes with a little decoration.
Just a bit though, Don't overdo!

PRODUCE
Accessorize your meals with garnishes from the produce section.

PARSLEY AND MINT LEAVES
Fabulous garnishes! Always keep a little of each on hand.

CILANTRO
A bit spicier than parsley, but very popular.

LETTUCE
Line your serving dish with leaf lettuce. Use a variety of colors.

RED CABBAGE
With the stem part as the bottom, cut the top off and hollow out a bowl to serve dip in.
Serve with veggies on a platter lined with lettuce leaves.

RADISH FLOWERS
I can't make them, but they make a nice garnish.
For a party, order them from your grocer already prepared.
Or, if you want to go crazy and spend the time –
check out FLO'S CORNER for creative ways to slice your vegetables.

ORANGE SLICES
This one even I can do. Slice, twist, lay on plate.

TWIST OF LEMON
Same deal as orange slices.

GRAPES
A small cluster on the side of a plate looks pretty and tastes good, too.
You can wet the grapes and dip them in sugar for that frosted look.
If you have your kids do this, tell them to use water, not spit.

THOSE CUTE LITTLE PAPER UMBRELLAS YOU SEE STICKING OUT OF FANCY DRINKS ON THE BEACH
Go crazy! Use them on everything.
Visit a party store and pick up a few fun things to keep around
for those special occasions.

FLOWERS
Flowers in vases on the table and around the house are a must. Your grocer also should have packaged edible flowers in the produce section that you can add to any dish. Don't use fresh cut flowers in your food unless you know which ones aren't poisonous. Call your local poison control center with questions. Remember those little, old ladies in that movie who started a garden of their own by serving arsenic laden tea to lonely gentlemen?
Well, arsenic may have a very nice flower, but it's not the best idea for a garnish.

ACCESSORIZE YOUR KITCHEN TOO!
Just because you don't cook a lot, doesn't mean you can't let people think that you do.
Bright colored fruit and vegetables look great in a bowl or basket,
displayed on the counter. After the party, you can use them on you!
See our "FOR THE BOD" section.

DIPS

&

HORS D'OEUVRES

When I'm invited to a party, the hostess always asks me to bring the dip. You'd think by now, they'd know her name.

RANCH DIP

Ranch Dip mix and 16-oz sour cream. I substitute plain yogurt for sour cream for a dip that's easier to digest. You can also use half yogurt and half sour cream.

ONION DIP

French Onion Soup and Dip mix - Works best with sour cream or half sour cream and half regular, plain yogurt. Nonfat yogurt substitution is very noticeable with this dip mix.

SPINACH DIP

Spinach or Vegetable Dip mix - Most of these dip mixes are found in the soup section of the grocery store. Follow directions for spinach dip on the package. Hollow out a round of sourdough bread to make bread bowl. Spoon the dip into the bread bowl and place it in a lined basket. Arrange French bread slices (pre-sliced from the bakery) and vegetable flavored crackers in the basket, around the dip. Serve with a knife for spreading.

BEAN DIP

1 can of refried beans (or vegetarian chili)
1 Tbsp. garlic (powdered or crushed)
¼ cup grated cheese

Option - Spike it with salsa!

Pour the beans into a bowl and stir in the garlic. Top with cheese. Microwave on high for 2 minutes (until bubbly). Garnish with chopped green onion and cilantro.

SALSA

Health food stores have fabulous fresh prepared salsa without a lot of preservatives. If you have the time, pick some up. You can snazz it up with chopped cilantro, green onions and garlic. Here's another way to make it:

4 diced tomatoes
1 small onion (diced)
1 bunch cilantro (chopped)
6 green onions (chopped)
½ tsp. crushed garlic
1 jar or container of mild salsa

Mix together. It makes a delicious mild salsa.

If you'd like it hotter, add diced chili peppers. Don't touch your eyes after cutting them, though. You can wash your hands in lemon juice to remove the hot chili pepper oil.

Tasting Tip: If your salsa makes your ears steam, eat a tortilla chip to cool your mouth off. Bread works too. Drinking water will only make it worse. You can make your hot salsa milder by adding more tomatoes and another jar of prepared mild salsa.

Oh, this recipe doesn't call for jalapenos!

GUACAMOLE

I usually order mine from the taco bar down the street. They even deliver. But if you really want to make yours, here's a recipe:

4 avocados
½ cup salsa
¼ cup finely chopped onion
½ cup cilantro
Dash of hot sauce
Dash of cumin
¼ tsp. chili powder
Juice from 1 lemon
Garlic powder (to taste. I add a lot.)

Mix the ingredients together. Season to taste. Serve chunky - it's less work.

For parties - Double the recipe, except for the lemon juice. One lemon is enough.

Tip - If you are making it to serve later, don't mix in the lemon juice. Squeeze it on top to keep the guacamole from turning brown. Refrigerate. Stir immediately before serving.

Another way to keep the guacamole from turning brown is to spread a layer of salsa on top or put an avocado pit in the bowl.

DELICIOUS HAM DIP

8 oz. pkg. cream cheese
6 oz. can deviled ham
1 pkg. dry ranch salad dressing mix
½ cup diced green bell pepper
½ cup diced tomato
2 green onions, chopped
2 cups shredded cheddar cheese

Mix and refrigerate for 2 hours.

Form into a ball or log and roll in dry roasted sunflower seeds. Garnish with parsley.

Serve with your favorite crackers.

FLO'S FAMOUS THAT'S NACHO DIP

A must for pot luck's. This one is a meal in itself and serves a crowd - or one teenager.

1 lb. ground meat
1 onion
1 cup grated jack cheese
1 cup grated cheddar cheese
2 Tbsp. hot sauce
1 Tbsp. crushed garlic
17-oz. can refried or vegetarian beans
7-oz. can green chili salsa
4-oz. can diced green chiles

Garnish:
Guacamole
Sour cream
Diced tomatoes
Green onions (chopped)
Diced black olives

Fry the meat and onions. Drain off the fat. Spray a 13 x 9-inch glass baking dish with low-fat cooking spray. Spread the beans in the pan. Add the meat and onion mixture, then sprinkle hot sauce over the mixture. Sprinkle the green chiles and cheese. Spoon salsa over top.

Bake at 400 for 20-30 minutes.

Cool about 5 minutes. Spread sour cream, then guacamole, over hot dip. Garnish with diced tomatoes, green onion and black olives.

Serve warm with tortilla chips and more salsa.

DARLENE'S ARTICHOKE DIP

1 cup cream cheese
1 cup mayonnaise
14-oz. artichoke hearts (drained)
1 cup Parmesan cheese
1 round bread loaf

Mix cream cheese, mayonnaise and Parmesan together. Chop and add artichoke hearts. Hollow out a round loaf of bread. Save the lid and inner bread parts. Fill the loaf with dip. Place lid on top. Wrap in foil and bake at 350 for 45 to 60 minutes.

Serve in a basket, lined with a dinner napkin with crackers and bread.

SALMON SPREAD

8 oz. pkg. cream cheese (softened)
⅓ cup plain low-fat yogurt
2 Tbsp. milk
1 tsp. dill
½ tsp. lemon-pepper seasoning
6½ oz. can boneless salmon (drained)
3 Tbsp. finely grated carrot
3 Tbsp. finely chopped green onion or chives

Combine ingredients in bowl and beat until smooth. Transfer into a small serving dish. Cover and chill for 3 hours or overnight.

Serve with crackers or toasted sour dough bread rounds.

DARLENE'S SUN-DRIED TOMATO SPREAD

2 pkgs. cream cheese
½ cup sun-dried tomatoes (marinated, drained and finely chopped)
2 tsp. garlic or 3 med. cloves, crushed

Mix together and chill overnight. Fabulous on crackers!

DILL DIP

⅓ cup sour cream
⅓ cup mayonnaise
1½ tsp. dill weed
1 tsp. seasoned salt
1 Tbsp. finely chopped onion
1 Tbsp. parsley flakes

Mix together, grab a bag of chips and sit down.

For parties, triple the recipe. Serve with a vegetable platter or chicken wings.

VEGETARIAN NINE LAYER DIP

Refried beans or vegetarian chili
Grated cheddar cheese
Guacamole
Sour cream
Diced olives
Tomatoes
Green onions
Cilantro
Salsa

Spread beans in large shallow pan. Cover with grated cheese. Nuke on high for 5 minutes, until the beans and cheese bubble.

Spread a layer of guacamole on top. Add a layer of sour cream. Sprinkle layers of chopped tomatoes, green onions, and cilantro. Top with salsa. Garnish with diced olives. Serve with tortilla chips.

AUNT DOROTHY'S DEVILED EGGS

12 hard boiled eggs
Mustard
Mayonnaise
Salt & pepper to taste
Paprika
Parsley

Remove the eggshells and slice the eggs in half. Gently scoop the egg yolks into a bowl. Add about 1 teaspoon mustard and enough mayonnaise to moisten. Season with salt and pepper. Spoon mixture into the center of each egg. Sprinkle paprika over the top. Garnish your serving dish with parsley.

CURRIED CHICKEN CHEESE BALL

2 - 8 oz. pkgs. cream cheese softened
1½ cups boiled chopped chicken
¼ cup chopped celery
¼ cup chopped onion
¼ tsp. curry powder (or to taste)
1 tsp. steak sauce

Mix well. Shape into a ball. Cover with parsley and sliced almonds. Press parsley and almonds gently into the cheese ball.

Serve on a pretty plate with crackers.

HAM ROLLS

Definitely a popular party treat in our house. You can add just about anything to the cream cheese filling for an addicting treat. Here are two of our favorite variations:

MILD HAM ROLLS

3 - 8-oz. pkgs. cream cheese
1 pkg. dry ranch dressing mix
⅓ cup finely minced radish
2 or 3 minced green onions
1½ Tbsp. chopped olives
1 pack of 4 x 6 ham slices

SPICY HAM ROLLS

1 pack of 4 x 6 ham slices
2 - 8-oz. pkgs. cream cheese (softened)
1 can diced green chiles
3 green onions diced
1½ Tbsp. chopped black olives
½ cup grated cheddar cheese
Hot sauce (to taste)
Seasoned salt or salt substitute

Mix together and spread on ham slices. Roll up longways and chill about 20 minutes. Cut each roll into six 1" pieces. Insert toothpicks. Place on a bed of lettuce leaves. Garnish the ends of the toothpicks with olive or pimento.

Chill until you're ready to serve.

BRUSCETTA

4 Roma tomatoes in chunks
1 Tbsp. crushed garlic
Fresh basil, cut up
½ small red onion (diced)
Olive oil to moisten
Champagne vinegar
A dash of Balsamic vinegar
Salt & pepper

Option: Add crumbled mozzarella cheese!

Mix tomatoes, garlic, basil and diced onion together. Shake in olive oil (just a little), champagne vinegar and balsamic vinegar. Add salt & pepper to taste. Chill and serve with crackers or dry toast.

Health tip: You can substitute apple cider vinegar for the champagne vinegar if you'd like. It will change the taste, but it's still good.

When we first got together, Herb and I drove up the coast for an impromptu romantic getaway. I packed a picnic basket for us to nibble on while watching the sunset. You know, the usual *"use your hands it's more sensual"* type fare ~ bruscetta, crusty bread, grapes, cheese, wine and bottled water. Well, I won't give you the details, but we were smiling for weeks!

MARGARET'S CHEESE THINGS
Fabulous on a brunch buffet!

12 eggs
3 cups grated cheddar cheese
3 Tbsp. diced green chiles
Dash of hot sauce
All purpose seasoning

Beat the eggs. Stir in cheese, chiles, hot sauce and seasoning.

Pour into a greased baking dish or cookie sheet. Mixture should be less than 1" deep.

Bake at 350 for 5 to 10 minutes, until firm and golden. Do not brown. Cut into squares and serve.

RANCH DRUMETTES

24 drumettes or chicken wings
10 oz. pkg. of ranch dressing mix
2 oz. hot sauce
3 Tbsp. vinegar
1 tsp. paprika
⅓ cup margarine (melted)

Blend hot sauce, vinegar and margarine together.

Coat wings in liquid mixture. Dredge them in the dry dressing mix. Sprinkle with paprika.

Bake at 400 for 25 to 30 minutes. Turn wings and bake at 450 for an additional 20 to 25 minutes. Serve with Ranch dip and celery stalks.

CRAB STUFFED MUSHROOMS

Large mushroom caps

Filling:
Crabmeat (drained)
Bread crumbs
Mayonnaise (just enough to moisten)
Diced green onions
Dash of hot sauce
All purpose seasoning

Option: Sprinkle with Parmesan if desired.

Wash well. Remove the stem from each mushroom.

Mix ingredients together. Spoon mixture into mushroom caps and place on ungreased cookie sheet. Bake at 350 for 12 to 15 minutes. Serve hot.

PAPA'S SHRIMP COCKTAILS

Bay shrimp
Cocktail sauce
Diced celery

Snazz up the cocktail sauce with:
1 Tsp. horseradish
½ Tsp. dry mustard
2 dashes of black pepper

Option: Add finely diced cilantro to sauce or a squeeze of fresh lemon juice.

Prepare a shrimp cocktail for each guest. Any type of glass will do as long as it's not too tall. Special shrimp cocktail glasses are the best, though. If you have some, add some crushed ice to the bottom glass, then place the cocktail glass inside.

Place about ¼ cup of diced celery at the bottom of each shrimp cocktail glass. Top with shrimp

Mix cocktail sauce and seasonings. Spoon on top of shrimp.

Delicious!

HOLD THE PHONE! *Don't miss out on these incredible **"I-don't-care-what's-in-it-I'm-eating-it-anyway"** recipes. Check 'em out in the Udder Decadence section!*

CHILI CHEESE DIP
A party favorite.
See the Udder Decadence section.

CRAB DIP
Oh my gosh!
See the Udder Decadence section.

MEALS YOU CAN MAKE
IN LESS TIME
THAN IT TAKES TO DO YOUR HAIR

MEALS YOU CAN MAKE IN LESS TIME THAN IT TAKES TO DO YOUR HAIR

We know what our priorities are, now don't we?

LOW-FAT CHINESE CHICKEN SALAD

1 pre-cooked chicken
1 bunch of cilantro (chopped)
Bean sprouts
Lettuce (fresh or packaged)
Green onions (chopped)
Sliced almonds or water chestnuts
Tomato (sliced)
Red cabbage (packaged, shredded)
Sesame seeds

Options: Mandarin oranges, bell pepper
grated carrots, chow mein noodles

In a large bowl, combine lettuce, cilantro, bean sprouts, green onion, tomato, red cabbage and almonds or water chestnuts.

Tear the chicken into shreds - (This is really fun after a bad day at work). Arrange the chicken on your salad.

Sprinkle sesame seeds over salad. Serve with seasoned rice vinegar or bottled dressing. For other dressing ideas, see the *Rabbit Food* section.

Amounts of everything depend on the number of people you're serving. Leftovers will stay fresh in the fridge as long as you don't put dressing on them. I usually rinse off the lettuce and red cabbage ~ just to make sure nobody hitched a ride in the packaging line. (*Mmm! These red spotted things are crunchy!*)

This salad is great with warm pumpernickel rolls!

Preparation time: about 15 minutes.

THE FIFTEEN MINUTE ITALIAN
Pasta with Marinara Sauce, Salad & Garlic Bread

PASTA

Your favorite pasta
Water
Your favorite marinara sauce
        (or whatever's available)
A little extra garlic

Spaghetti test - throw a piece against the refrigerator. If it sticks, it's done. If it falls off, cook it some more and try again.

Shell pasta test - Ask your husband to try it. Watch his face.

Pour 4 to 5 cups of water into a pan. Bring to a boil.

While that's working, open a jar or plastic container of your favorite marinara sauce and pour it into a sauce pan. Add a dash or two of garlic. Cook over medium heat, stirring occasionally.

Add **pasta** to boiling water and stir. Let it cook for a few minutes or until it is soft throughout.

Drain pasta, mix with marinara sauce.

Place into serving bowl and garnish with more parsley and Parmesan.

PASTA WITHOUT MARINARA SAUCE

Same as the Fifteen Minute Italian, but instead of marinara, drain the pasta and throw it back in the pan. Add a little **butter**, a lot of **Parmesan cheese, garlic powder** and **parsley flakes**. Mix together and serve. *Option*: Add **pesto** instead of butter. *Another option*: Switch to French food, I hear it takes longer.

GARLIC BREAD

1 loaf Italian or sour dough bread
Butter or margarine
2 Tbsp. crushed garlic
Parmesan cheese
Parsley flakes

Microwave a half a stick of margarine for 30 seconds (until soft but not runny) Add 2 tbsp. crushed garlic (I get mine in a jar, but you can substitute powdered or fresh if you'd like). Stir garlic into margarine and spread lightly over sliced bread. Sprinkle with Parmesan and parsley flakes.

Place on a cookie sheet or sheet of aluminum foil. Bake for about 5 minutes or until edges of bread start to brown. You can broil it if you're in a hurry, but watch it closely. Remove it when it begins to bubble. Do not overcook.

Line a basket with a linen napkin. Place garlic bread in basket and serve.

SALAD

1 pre-fab salad
Some type of dressing

Take your **salad** out of it's plastic container, rinse it thoroughly, drain or whizz it in one of those salad spinners - then place it in an attractive serving bowl. Add salad tongs and place on the table.

See the *"Rabbit Food"* section for salad dressing ideas or use your favorite bottled dressing.

WOK CHICKEN

Chicken strips
Red & green bell pepper
1 sliced onion
3 cloves or 2 Tbsp. garlic
1 cup bean sprouts
1 cup snow peas
½ cup water chestnuts
Teriyaki sauce
Grated ginger (just a pinch)

Total time:
About 7 minutes.

Another way to
walk a chicken.

Spray a frying pan or wok with low fat cooking spray. Saute garlic and onions over medium-high heat. Add chicken.

Cook for 3 minutes, stirring occasionally. Stir in bell pepper, water chestnuts, snow peas and bean sprouts.

Cook for 2 minutes. Sprinkle with teriyaki or low-salt soy sauce. Serve.

Time-saver tip: Get your veggies from the salad bar already cut up.

Variations: Add Broccoli, Zucchini, Yellow Squash, String Beans and /or your favorite vegetables.

Stir in fresh grated ginger while cooking.

EASY CURRY CHICKEN
Toss it in the oven and you're done!

1 package boneless skinless chicken
½ cup honey
¼ cup prepared mustard
1 Tbsp. curry powder (or more to taste)

Spray a pan with low fat cooking spray. Rinse, then add the chicken.

Mix honey, mustard and curry together and pour over chicken.

Bake at 375 for 45 - 60 minutes. Serve over cooked rice.

Preparation time: Less than 5 minutes.

STEAMED FISH

2 thin filets of your favorite fish
Broccoli (1 bunch cutup)
½ red onion (sliced)
Garlic (1 clove or 1 tsp.)
Zucchini (1 sliced)
Yellow squash (1 sliced)
1 cup water
2 lemons

Total time: About 7 minutes.

Pour water into large pan or pot. Add garlic to water. Place vegetable steamer attachment in pan. Add vegetables. Place fish on top. Season with all purpose seasoning. Squeeze 1 lemon over fish. Cover. Bring to a boil. Cook about 5 minutes.

The Fish should be even in color and flake easily when touched with a fork.
Serve over rice. Garnish with lemon slices and diced parsley.

PITA PIZZA

Pita bread
Marinara sauce
Red onion (sliced)
Bell pepper (sliced)
Eggplant (thinly sliced)
Tomato (sliced)
Mozzarella cheese (or low fat substitute, grated)
Parmesan cheese (grated)

Total time: About 5 minutes.

Preheat oven to 425. Spread the marinara sauce on pita bread. Layer with vegetables. Cover vegetables with mozzarella cheese. Sprinkle a little Parmesan cheese on top.

Bake until the cheese melts and the marinara begins to bubble. Cut into quarters and serve.

Options: Substitute some of your favorite pizza toppings or a pre-made pizza crust.

Grill it: Saute the bell pepper, onion and mushroom before placing them on the pizza crust. Top with cheese and a little extra marinara, bake until cheese melts.

Total time: 7-10 minutes.

CHICKEN DIJON

Chicken (1 package, deboned, skinless)
1 onion (sliced)
2 Tbsp. mustard
¼ cup white wine
2 Tbsp. capers (optional)

Rinse chicken and throw in pan. Add onion and saute for about 3 minutes turning once. Add mustard and wine.

Simmer over medium-low heat until chicken is thoroughly cooked. *(If you're in a hurry, use thin pieces of chicken, they cook faster.)* Garnish with capers before serving.

Total time: About 7 minutes.

PITA POCKETS

Pita bread
Mayonnaise or non-fat yogurt
Mustard
Avocado
Lettuce
Tomato
Turkey
Alfalfa sprouts

Slice one end of pita bread to open. Spread mayonnaise and mustard inside. Add other ingredients and cut in half. Serve.

Total time: About 5 minutes

HOT POCKET

Pita bread
Zucchini (sliced)
Marinara sauce
Cheese (grated)
Parmesan cheese

Spread marinara sauce inside the pita bread. Add sliced zucchini and grated cheese. Sprinkle with all purpose seasoning. Bake at 350 until cheese melts and marinara sauce begins to bubble. Cut in half. Sprinkle with Parmesan cheese and enjoy!

Total time: About 5 minutes

Option: Add cooked Italian or turkey sausage.

CHICKEN SALAD SANDWICH

Pre-cooked chicken
Finely chopped celery
Cilantro (chopped)
Red bell pepper (chopped)
Mayonnaise (just enough to moisten)
1 Tbsp. mustard
Dash of curry powder
Dash of celery salt

Preparation time: About 7 minutes.

Remove skin and bones from chicken. Cut the meat into cubes. Mix in other ingredients. Spoon the chicken salad on sliced bread and top with another slice. Smoosh together gently and cut sandwich in half.

OR -

Grab the bowl and a box of crackers and go sit down.

PREFAB PASTA
This recipe works best with a vegetable pasta, like pasta primavera.

Prepared pasta from the deli
1 jar of artichoke hearts (drained)
Bell pepper (sliced)
Pesto sauce
2 tomatoes (chopped)
Red onion (sliced chunky)
1 Tbsp. garlic (crushed)

Preparation time: About 5 minutes.

Heat the pesto sauce in the microwave for about 30 seconds. Drain the oil from the pesto sauce. (*A strainer works well for this.*)

Dump your pasta into a pretty bowl. Add the other ingredients. Toss thoroughly. Garnish with a little Parmesan cheese and chopped parsley. Serve with garlic bread or hot rolls.

Option: Heat it for a minute or two in the microwave before serving.

EASY QUES·YOURDILLAS

Tortillas
Grated cheddar cheese
Beans (refried or vegetarian chili)
Red onion (sliced)
Tomatoes (sliced)
Bell pepper (sliced)
Green onion (chopped)
Cilantro (chopped)
Salsa

Preparation time: Less than 5 minutes.

Place a tortilla on a plate. Add beans, veggies and cheese. Lay another tortilla on top. Nuke for 1 minute. Cut into quarters. Serve.

Tip from Dish :
Pre-fab your veggies!
Get them from the salad bar.

Tip from Flo: Melt the cheese, but don't let it bubble too much. Overcooked cheese is hard, crusty and not very appetizing.

Dish: Wow! That party was so long ago. I thought you'd have forgotten about it by now.

Flo: Believe me, I've tried.

ONE-DISH-
AND-YOU'RE-DONE-DINNERS

ONE-DISH-
AND-YOU'RE-DONE-DINNERS
All the food groups in one pan. Easy clean-up!

JOHN'S FABULOUS MACARONI & CHEESE
Kids will eat it, too!

1 pkg. macaroni & cheese
Milk
Mushrooms (sliced)
Broccoli tops
Zucchini (sliced)
Bell pepper (chopped)
Steak or chicken (cubed, cooked)

Saute the veggies and meat together. Set aside. Follow the directions on the macaroni & cheese package. (You can leave out the butter if you'd like.)

Add the veggies and meat to the macaroni & cheese and cook over medium heat, stirring constantly for 2 more minutes. Serve.

VEGETABLE MARINARA

Zucchini (sliced)
Yellow squash (sliced)
Eggplant (chopped)
Onion (sliced)
Bell pepper (chopped)
Parsley (finely chopped)
1 container of marinara sauce
½ Tbsp. garlic (crushed)
Seasoning (all purpose)

Spray a pan with low-fat cooking spray. Saute the vegetables for about 2 minutes, stirring occasionally. Season with your favorite all purpose or Italian seasoning.

Add marinara sauce. Cook over medium heat until thoroughly bubbly. Serve over any type of cooked pasta.

Serve with garlic bread or fresh hot rolls!

VEGETABLE LASAGNA

Step 1
Zucchini (sliced)
Onion (chopped)
Bell pepper (chopped)
Spinach (10 oz. pkg., frozen, chopped)
Garlic (3 tsp.)

Toss the ingredients into a blender and buzz on medium speed until blended to a coarse pulp.

Step 2
Lasagna noodles (cooked)
Marinara sauce (2 containers or 4 cups)
Ricotta cheese (1 container)

Layer a baking dish with cooked lasagna noodles, marinara sauce, 1/3 of the vegetable mixture and ricotta cheese.

Then, make 2 more layers of the same.

Step 3
Mozzarella cheese
Parmesan cheese

Add another layer of lasagna noodles and spread the remaining marinara sauce over them.

Sprinkle mozzarella and Parmesan cheeses abundantly on top.

Bake for 30 minutes. Garnish with parsley. Serve with garlic bread.

Option: Add sliced eggplant or cooked ground turkey meat.

VEGETABLE CASSEROLE
Remember, buy your veggies already cut up.

**1 bunch or pkg. broccoli
        (fresh or frozen, chopped)
1 pkg. spinach (frozen, chopped)
1 jar artichoke hearts
        (packed in water, drained)
1 pkg. peas (frozen)
1 onion (chopped)
2 zucchini or yellow squash (chopped)
1 small can diced green chiles (diced)
3 eggs
1 pkg. grated cheddar cheese
2 Tbsp. water
All purpose seasoning**

Pre-heat the oven to 350. Spray a baking dish with low-fat cooking spray.

Rinse and drain the vegetables , then layer in the baking pan. Beat the eggs, water, chiles, cheese and seasoning together. Spread the mixture over the vegetables. *(I usually poke it in with a fork, then sprinkle a little more grated cheese on top).*

Bake for 30 minutes. It should be very bubbly, but not brown.

Options: You can substitute any of the vegetables for whatever you've got in the kitchen.

RICE

I'm not very good with rice. People who eat my rice say, "Mmm...this tastes very healthy." Then they excuse themselves for a few minutes. Take my word for it: If you want to make rice, get your recipe from a different book.

Or better yet -- Buy it already made and jazz it up with a tiny bit of finely chopped parsley sprinkled over the top. Hide those containers!

Tip from Flo: Get a rice cooker!
Dish: Preferably a cute one.

OK - I'll give you one recipe for rice -
You'll have to take off those press-on nails for this one.

RICE

1 part rice
2 parts water
automatic rice cooker or pan with lid.

First - Measure your ingredients:

Rice Cooker - Follow manufacturer directions to measure and cook.

Pan - Touch the tip of your finger to the inside bottom of pan. Fill rice to 1st bottom knuckle. Pour water to the top knuckle (where your finger meets your hand).

Cover. Bring to boil. I was told not to peek at the rice. It lets the steam out. Wait until the lid starts to jump up and down, then lower the heat to a simmer.

I don't know how long you should simmer it. I'm not a great rice cooker. I usually cook it to the point between when the rice sucks up all the water and before the pan burns. Moisten it with some type of sauce.

SOMEBODY ELSE'S RECIPE FOR SUSHI RICE

Combine in saucepan -
1 cup short grain rice
2 cups cold water

Bring to a rapid boil for 5 minutes. Don't open the lid. *(See? What'd I tell ya)*
Reduce heat to medium and cook for 10 minutes. Then, reduce heat to low and cook for 15 minutes.

(This recipe sounds like one of those math questions: If the rice went from cold and hard directly to hot and sticky, how much time would have elapsed? Actually, if your rice went from cold and hard to hot and sticky, I want to meet your rice cooker! Is he available? Just kidding. I love my Herb. He doesn't do rice either, but he's cute.)

When rice is done, spread it out on a cookie sheet to cool. Heat 3 Tbsp. plus 2 tsp. of sugar until dissolved. Add 1/4 cup rice vinegar. Pour over rice and mix. You're now ready to make sushi!

SUSHI
My favorite way to do sushi is to eat out!

My second favorite way is to buy it from the grocer. Arrange it on a platter. Garnish with the ginger and wasabi that came in the cute little plastic box. Serve low-salt soy sauce on the side. Orange slices for dessert. But, if you really want to make it, here are a few recipes:

REIKO'S PHILADELPHIA ROLL
Fabulous hors d' oeuvre!

Cream cheese
Smoked salmon
Thin cucumber strips
Nori seaweed sheets (toasted)
Sushi rice

Option: Add a thin slice of carrot for color.

Lay seaweed on a piece of plastic wrap. Spread rice on seaweed. Layer cream cheese, salmon and cucumber. Use the plastic wrap to help roll it up. Cut into 1" pieces. Remove the plastic wrap. Arrange on a plate with soy sauce.

58

SASHIMI

Fresh ahi or high quality tuna
      (tell your butcher it's for sashimi)
Low salt soy sauce
Fresh prepared ginger
      (buy it prepared from your grocer)
Wasabi
      (Prepared Japanese horseradish)

Slice the tuna into 2" long 1/4" thick strips. Cut at an angle with the grain of the fish. Arrange them on a platter.

Place the ginger and wasabi in little mounds on the platter. Garnish with thinly sliced lemon and carrot strips.

Serve with soy sauce and individual dipping bowls.

CALIFORNIA ROLL

Crabmeat
Cucumber (sliced lengthwise in quarters)
Avocado (sliced into strips)
Sushi rice
Seaweed

If you have a sushi roller, cover it with a sheet of plastic wrap (to keep the rice from squishing out of the grooves). If not use a sheet of wax paper. Place seaweed square on the roller.

Add ½ cup rice and flatten it over the surface of the seaweed. Down the center of the square add crabmeat, avocado and cucumber. Roll up, remove from plastic or wax paper and cut into 1" pieces.

Serve with soy sauce, wasabi and ginger on the side.

Tip from Flo ~ Always cover your bamboo sushi roller with plastic wrap (tape to secure) to keep the seaweed from sticking.

CHICKEN WITH VEGETABLES

1 pkg. chicken (boneless, skinless)
1 potato
½ cup fresh green beans
½ cup carrots
¼ cup red onion
½ cup yellow zucchini
2 envelopes chicken soup mix*
⅔ cup fat free chicken broth

Spray pan with low fat cooking spray. Cut chicken and brown over medium heat. Stir in sliced vegetables. Add seasonings and chicken broth. Cover and simmer for 45 minutes.

One Dish Option: Add 1 cup of water and 1 cup of rice. Cover and

*Optional seasonings: Poultry seasoning, celery seed, coriander, bouquet garni.

EGGPLANT PARMESAN

Eggplant
Mozzarella cheese
Parmesan cheese
Marinara sauce
Parsley
Good company

Spray a baking dish with low fat cooking spray. Cut the eggplant into 1" thick slices.

Layer the eggplant in the baking dish. Cover with marinara sauce. Top with mozzarella cheese. Add another layer if you'd like. Cover with marinara sauce and top with mozzarella cheese.

Bake at 350 for 20 - 30 minutes. Remove from oven. Sprinkle with Parmesan cheese. Garnish with chopped parsley. Serve with garlic bread and great music.

QUICK FROZEN ENTREE

1 frozen entree (your favorite)
1 glass of good wine (also your favorite)

Sip the wine to make sure it is good. Remove the frozen entree from it's package and microwave until done.

Have some more wine. Remove the hot entree from the microwave and peel back the plastic covering. Serve.

Option: Non-alcoholic wine will do just as well.

PIZZA SANDWICH

1 loaf of brown & serve french bread
½ lb. ground meat
2 Tbsp. grated Parmesan cheese
A dash of pepper
2 Tbsp. chopped black olives
1 tsp. chopped green onion
3 oz. tomato paste
Grated mozzarella cheese

Cut the loaves into halves, horizontally. Combine all ingredients except the cheese. Spread ½ of the mixture on each loaf of bread.

Place the bread, meat side up, on an ungreased cookie sheet. Bake at 350 for 25 minutes.

Remove from oven. Sprinkle cheese over the top and bake for 5 more minutes. (Or until cheese is melted, but not brown.)

Take out of the oven and cut loaves diagonally into individual servings.

GOULASH
One dish, two pans ~ it's still easy

Lean ground turkey meat
2 cups marinara sauce (1 jar)
1 onion (chopped)
½ package frozen corn
1 package pasta shells
Garlic (2 Tbsp. crushed or to taste)
All purpose seasoning

Total time: About 20 minutes

In a pot, combine water and pasta. Bring to a boil.   Cook until pasta is done.

While that's working, saute ground turkey and onions in a large pan. Add marinara sauce, corn and spices. Simmer for about 10 minutes. Mix in the cooked pasta.

Serve with crusty Italian bread or rolls.

Note: This goulash is really good, but the combination of foods may not digest well. To eliminate any after-dinner unpleasantries, leave out the turkey. Or, just enjoy it. Have seconds! If anyone notices an terrible odor coming from your direction, stare at the dog in disgust.

CARNE ASADA

Top sirloin steak (or ask your butcher what they recommend)
Fresh lime juice
Beer
Garlic
Oregano
Tiny pinch of chili pepper
Dash of soy sauce

Marinate meat in mixture for at least 15 minutes. One hour is better.

Barbeque and serve taco style.

Option: Serve in a bowl over beans and rice. Garnish with chopped onion, tomato and cilantro. Substitute chicken for beef.

Buy it already made from your nearby store or restaurant. Hide those containers!

FISH ON THE ROCKS

Filets of fish
2 cups rice
Vegetable or fat-free chicken broth
1 large onion (chopped)
6 green onions (diced)
4 large tomatoes (diced)
2 Tbsp. crushed garlic
1 Tbsp. olive oil
1 lemon
6 mushrooms (sliced)
Dash of pepper
Dash of cayenne
½ tsp. paprika
¼ cup cilantro (chopped)

Combine the rice and chopped onions. Spread mixture inside a large baking dish. Lay the fish fillets on top. Add broth.

In a bowl, combine tomatoes, garlic, olive oil and seasonings. Set aside.

Place mushrooms and green onions on fish. Squeeze the juice from one lemon over fish. Add cilantro. Spoon ½ of the tomato mixture over fish. Sprinkle with paprika.

Cover. Bake at 400 for 30 minutes. Garnish with more tomato mixture and green onion.

TACOS

1 pkg. ground chicken or turkey
Finely chopped vegetables:
      carrots
      green onions
      broccoli
      mushrooms
      cilantro
      tomatoes

Cook together over medium heat.

Add:
Dash of chili powder
1 Tbsp. garlic
½ dash of cumin
Cornstarch and water

Saute for 5 more minutes.

Stir in:
½ cup salsa
Dash of coriander
Dash of garlic powder
Bouquet gari
½ cup diced tomatoes
¼ cup honey

Cook for another 2 minutes.

Serve with no-lard, fat-free tortillas, low fat grated cheese, chopped lettuce, guacamole and salsa.

Note: Adding the cornstarch will reduce the chances of the taco meat dripping on your pants. Mix the cornstarch with cool water, then add it to the meat. Otherwise, it will make lumps.

CORI'S CHICKEN ENCHILADAS

Sauce:
1 can cream of chicken soup
1 cup sour cream
Diced green chiles
Dash of bouquet gari
⅛ tsp. cumin
Dash of coriander
2 dashes of garlic powder
Dash of onion Powder

Mix together over medium heat.

Chicken filling:
1 chicken

Boil and shred chicken (or tear apart a pre-cooked one).

Add:
½ cup sliced mushrooms
½ cup diced red bell pepper
½ cup cilantro
½ cup green onion
1 Tbsp. green chiles

Add to chicken and saute in margarine.

Heat 12 corn tortillas. Dip in sauce then place in baking dish. Add chicken filling and **grated jack cheese**. Roll and continue until pan is full. Pour remaining sauce over the enchiladas and top with jack cheese. Bake at 375 for 30 minutes until bubbly. Garnish with **avocado, salsa, cilantro** and fresh diced **tomato**.

In a hurry? Instead of rolling enchiladas ~ layer tortillas, chicken, sauce and cheese. Bake. *It all goes to the same place anyway.*

KITCHEN SINK BURRITOS

Step 1
1 pkg. chicken strips (boneless, skinless, cut up)
1 onion (chopped)
1 green bell pepper (sliced)
1 red bell pepper (sliced)
Cilantro (1 bunch, chopped)
1 tsp. garlic
½ tsp. cumin
½ tsp. chili powder
All purpose seasoning

Saute the ingredients together for about 5 minutes (or until the chicken is done).

Step 2
Tortillas (corn or flour)
Grated cheese (jack or cheddar)
Chopped tomato (chopped)
4 green onions (chopped)
Shredded lettuce
Salsa

Spoon the chicken mixture down the center of tortilla. Add cheese, tomato, onions, lettuce and salsa. Roll up and place on plates.

Garnish with a dollop of sour cream and guacamole. Sprinkle more salsa and cilantro on top.

Option: Add 1 or 2 cans of vegetarian chili to chicken mixture. Cook until bubbly.

Serve with *Flo's Famous "That's Nacho Dip!"* and tortilla chips.

Total time: About 25 minutes.

Provide crane service to move your guests to their cars after dinner.

STUFFED ZUCCHINI

8 large zucchinis
1 eggplant
2 tomatoes
1 bell pepper
1 onion
1 yellow squash
1 tsp. crushed garlic
1 tsp. all purpose seasoning
Parmesan cheese
1 container of marinara sauce
Sliced mozzarella or jack cheese

Slice zucchini horizontally and scoop out the insides being careful not to destroy the outer skin.

Chop other vegetables and toss them in the blender with the scooped out zucchini "meat". Add seasonings. Set blender on chop and turn on. Mixture should be finely chopped and well blended.

Place zucchini shells in a baking dish. Spoon vegetable mixture into zucchini shells. Cover with marinara sauce (*I like to add an extra bit of garlic to store-bought marinara sauce.*) Lay cheese on zucchini and sprinkle with Parmesan.

Bake at 350 for 25 minutes. Serve with pumpernickel rolls.

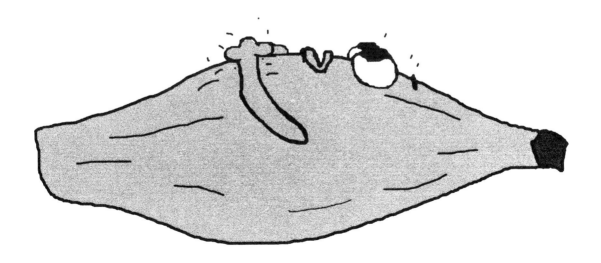

EASY ENTERTAINING

PRE-FAB IT!

For large parties, it's cheaper to make the food from scratch, but who has the time?
Here are some easy shortcuts I use at most of my parties:

WATERMELON BASKET

Dial the deli and order it!
At most stores you'll be able to choose a style and fruit type.

VEGETABLE TRAY

Go ahead! Pick one up.
Transfer the veggies to a basket or platter. Toss the tell-tale plastic container and add your own
dip. Be creative! Spoon the dip into a hollowed-out red cabbage or artichoke.
Garnish with radish flowers.

SHRIMP PLATTER

Easy! 1 bag of frozen shrimp, 1 jar cocktail sauce, 2 lemons.
Thaw the shrimp by placing the frozen package in the sink. Run cool water over it.
While the shrimp is thawing, pour the sauce into a bowl.
Arrange the thawed shrimp on a platter around the cocktail sauce.
Garnish with lemon slices and parsley.

If it won't be eaten right away, use a low bowl instead of the platter. Fill it with crushed ice
before arranging the shrimp. For a snazzier sauce, add a ½ tsp. of horseradish and/or mustard.

SALAD

Get your toppings from your grocer's Salad Bar. Use packaged lettuce (rinsed and drained).
I like to mix and match store-bought salads and salsa's. They make great toppings. Check out the
produce and deli sections of your store. Throw everything into a bowl with salad tongs. Serve the
dressing on the side so you can save the leftovers for tomorrow. Or, better yet, try one of those
gourmet ready-made salads. Dump it into a pretty bowl and serve as is. Why mess with perfection?

VISIT THE DELI

Pick up dishes to compliment your meal (*or to be your meal!*).
Pastas, dips, sliced cheeses and meats, toppings for salads.
It's turned into my favorite section of the store ~well, besides the cappuccino bar.

TURN FRUIT SALAD INTO A DESSERT

Serve it in wine glasses. Garnish with low-cal whipped cream or nonfat frozen yogurt.
Top with a fresh berry or mint leaf.

EASY SHORTCAKE

Cut angel food or pound cake into slices.
Layer with fruit and whipped cream (or nonfat frozen yogurt).
Drizzle juices from fruit over the top.
Garnish with a mint leaf, berry or thin slice of twisted orange.
Twisted orange...wasn't that a rock group in the 70's?

POT LUCK

This is always a good one. When the gals ask what they can bring ~ tell 'em!

71

LIGHT FARE DINNER PARTY
Pile on those carbs!

Step 1: Shop

DELI COUNTER
3 types of pasta - ask the person behind the deli counter how much pasta they recommend for the number of guests you are having.

SALAD BAR
Fill one plastic container with lettuce, and one with your favorite salad toppings. This should serve four to eight normal people. If your guests are from California, get more lettuce.

BAKERY SECTION
Pick up some dinner rolls and an angel food cake. One dinner roll for each person plus three extra in case you drop them on the floor.

PRODUCE SECTION
Cilantro or Italian parsley (for garnishes).

Also pick up ~
Bell pepper, tomato, avocado, cucumber, bananas and lemons. *Use them for decoration.* They'll look great in a bowl on the kitchen counter. Later, you can use them as Spa Treatments on you. See the "FOR THE BOD" section of this book.

FROZEN FOODS
Pick up a frozen berry mixture or your favorite frozen fruit. I usually go for strawberries, blackberries and blueberries. The leftovers are great in smoothies!

You'll also need ~
Pesto sauce
Grated Parmesan
Salad dressing
1 jar of artichoke hearts (packed in water)

Step 2: PREPARE

PASTA

Arrange all three pastas in sections of one large bowl or platter. Garnish with cilantro or Italian parsley. Serve a small dish of Parmesan on the side.

One of the pastas will undoubtedly be a vegetable type. Snazz this one up with the pesto, Parmesan and artichoke hearts.

Microwave the pesto sauce for 30 seconds on high. Drain most of the oil and discard it. Stir the pesto into the pasta. Add the drained artichoke hearts, a dash of garlic powder and stir together.

ROLLS

Place the rolls in a basket lined with a linen napkin.

SALAD

Rinse the salad and toppings. Drain or spin dry. Serve the salad in a nice bowl, dressing on the side.

DESSERT

Party food preparation time: About 30 minutes. For an added flare - Toss a thin slice of lemon into each water glass.

Slice the angel food cake into sections. Place a slice inside wine or parfait glasses (one for each guest).

Mix together in a bowl - frozen blackberries, blueberries and strawberries. Leave on counter to thaw. Drain most but not all of the juice. Sprinkle with cinnamon (2 Tbsp.) and stir together. Spoon the fruit mixture over the angel food cake and refrigerate. Just before serving, add a dollop of nonfat whipped topping or nonfat frozen yogurt. Garnish with berries.

"TRADITIONAL TURKEY DINNER" - Call your grocer & Order It!

Oh, you want to cook?

Turkey
Stuffing
Mashed Potatoes
Gravy
Cranberry Sauce
Green Salad
Carrot Salad
Dinner rolls

TURKEY & STUFFING

Preheat oven to 425

1 **Turkey**
1 **pkg. stuffing mix**
2 **cups chopped celery**
1 **cup chopped onion**
3 **Tbsp. poultry seasoning**
1 **Tbsp. sage**
1 **cup fat-free chicken broth**
½ **cup margarine or butter**

I usually make 4 times this much for a holiday dinner. My family loves stuffing...even mine!

Stuff the turkey at both ends. Place in pan. Rub canola or safflower oil lightly over skin to seal in the juices while cooking. Sprinkle with poultry seasoning. Cover.

Cook at 425 for 30 minutes then reduce heat to 325.

Bake about 20 minutes per pound or until turkey thermometer pops up. I usually cook mine until it falls apart. *Oh look! It's done!*

Health tip - Don't let the turkey sit out on the counter with the stuffing inside. Turkey can have an unhealthful biochemical reaction to the combination of warm stuffing and meat sitting out for more than a few minutes. It can make you very sick.

Scoop out all the stuffing as soon as you take the turkey out of the oven. I usually combine it with the extra stuffing I baked in a separate casserole dish. (Just follow the directions on the stuffing box.) Use the hot turkey drippings for gravy. Carve the turkey just before serving. Ask one of the men to do it. I don't know what it is about carving a turkey, but they seem to love it!

GRAVY

Turkey drippings
2 to 3 Tbsp. poultry seasoning
2 Tbsp. sage
½ tsp. all purpose seasoning
Flour (to desired consistency)
Water (for thinning, if necessary)

What are those, Dumplings?

Heat the turkey drippings in a pan over medium heat.

In a cup, mix a little flour and cold water. Stir together to get all the lumps out. Add flour mixture slowly to pan drippings, stirring constantly.

Stir in seasonings. Bring gravy to low boil then simmer until it reaches the desired consistency (a few minutes).

For a thicker gravy, add more flour/water mixture. Do not add flour directly to gravy unless you *want* lumps.

Tip from Flo: Always use cold water when adding flour or corn starch for thickening.

Tip from Dish: You'd be amazed at the lumps you get when you add the flour directly to the gravy. However, don't let a few lumps ruin your gravy...turn it into stew!

Tip from Flo: Or use a strainer.

Options: Stretch your gravy by adding packaged gravy mix and more water.

Some people like a little milk in their gravy. You can also use chicken broth instead of water or as a base.

MASHED POTATOES

Potatoes (1 bag, organic if possible)
Water
½ cup butter
¼ cup milk or water
Pepper
Salt (optional)

Scrub potatoes gently under water. Cut out any bad parts and discard. Slice potatoes into chunks leaving the skin on. Throw them into a large pot and fill it with water.

Bring to a boil, then cook over medium heat for about 20 minutes.

If you put a lid on it, it's sure to boil over and make a mess on your stove.

After cooking, drain most but not all of the water. Add butter or margarine, salt, pepper and milk.

Whip with a mixer until smooth. Spoon into a bowl and garnish with a huge dab of butter.

CRANBERRY SAUCE

Frozen blackberries
Frozen blueberries
Frozen strawberries
Frozen cherries
1 can whole cranberry sauce
1 small can crushed pineapple (drained)
3 Tbsp. cinnamon

A little goes a long way -- Save the leftovers -- it's good on toast the next morning.

See the **"What to do with those Leftovers"** section.

Thaw the frozen fruit. Place into a colander in the sink and drain.

If you'd like, put the colander in a bowl for the juice to drain into. You can use the juice later in a smoothie.

Place the drained fruit in a large bowl. Add the cranberry sauce and crushed pineapple. Sprinkle cinnamon on top. Mix together.

Refrigerate for 1 hour. Serve.

GREEN SALAD

You know the routine -- *Pre-Fab it!* Or go **Caesar** -- a bag of **lettuce, croutons, caesar dressing**. Rinse. Toss together in a bowl. Sprinkle with **Parmesan**.

CARROT SALAD

3 cups grated carrots
1 cup grated apple
1 cup raisins
1 Tbsp. cinnamon

Plump the raisins by marinating them in a glass of water .
Cold water - about 1 hour.
Warm water - about 5 minutes.

Drain. Mix the carrots, apples, raisins and cinnamon together.

Refrigerate until serving.

DELICIOUS HAM GLAZE

½ cup brown sugar
¼ cup honey
¼ cup molasses
¼ cup ketchup
¼ cup mustard

Bake ham at 325 for 1½ hours, uncovered. Mix ingredients together well. Brush over ham one half hour before it's done cooking.

OR -

Get a pre-cooked and sliced ham.   Nuke the glaze in the microwave in a loosely covered dish until hot. *Leave a hole for the air to escape so it doesn't explode.* Brush the glaze over your ham and serve the rest in a side dish. You may want to heat up your ham before guests arrive. If so, bake it uncovered with this delicious glaze.

CHICKEN A LA OLIVE
Cozy food your family will love!

1 Chicken (Cut up. Leave skin on.)
2 cups brown rice
2 cans fat free chicken broth
1 cup chopped onion
1 small can whole grapes
½ cup raisins
½ cup black olives (pitted)
¼ cup pimentos
½ cup sliced almonds
2 Tbsp. olive oil
2 Tbsp. poultry seasoning
1 Tbsp. crushed garlic
1 Tbsp. cinnamon
1 bay leaf
1 tsp. thyme

Preheat oven to 425. In a baking dish, combine olive oil, onion and seasonings. Heat for 2 minutes. Add rice. Brown for 10 minutes, stirring occasionally. Pour chicken broth into pan and add chicken.   Drain grapes, olives and pimentos and spread on top. Add raisins. Sprinkle seasonings and cover.

Reduce heat to 350 and bake for 1 ½ hours.

LEMON CHICKEN

6 chicken breast halves (skinless, boneless)
2 Tbsp. lemon juice
1 Tbsp. margarine or oil
1 Tbsp. chopped garlic
2 Tbsp. chopped parsley
2 Tbsp. grated Parmesan cheese

1 package chicken flavored rice
    (or pasta vermicelli mix)
1½ cup broccoli

Melt margarine in large skillet, add garlic and chicken. Cook over medium heat for 5 minutes on each side. Stir in lemon juice and parsley. Sprinkle with Parmesan.

Follow directions on packaged vermicelli mix. Add broccoli when you add the rice or pasta. Cover. Simmer until vermicelli is done.

Serve together. Garnish with parsley. Serve with a slice of lemon.
Option: Dust chicken in flour before cooking.

QUICK MUSTARD CHICKEN

I created this recipe before my last shopping day.
My husband "loves" those days --"What's for dinner?"
"I'm not sure yet, we'll see what it is when it's done!"

Chicken strips or breasts (skinless, boneless)
Mustard
Lemon

Saute chicken in pan. Squeeze the lemon and squirt the mustard over the chicken.

Stir, while cooking over medium heat for about 5 minutes, or until chicken is done. You can add sliced onion or mushrooms if you'd like.

Serve over rice or salad.

Option: Eat out.

CROCK POT PARTIES
&
NO MESS SOUPS

CROCK POT PARTIES & NO MESS SOUPS

In the morning, get out your crock pot and turn it on low.

VEGETABLE SOUP

1 bunch of celery (chopped)
1 lg. onion (chopped)
1 bunch parsley (chopped)
2 lg. cans tomatoes (cut)
3 cloves garlic
All purpose seasoning
Water

Add the ingredients to crock pot and cover. It will be ready at dinnertime.

Variations -
string beans
barley
kidney beans
pasta
tomato sauce
corn
zucchini
beans (soaked in
water the night before)
rice
carrots
lentils
peas
your favorite vegetables
cayenne pepper for zip

Serve with hot, crusty bread or whole wheat rolls.

CLAM CHOWDER

2 large cans clams (drained)
1 can clam juice
4 to 6 large potatoes (diced)
1 bunch of celery (chopped)
2 onions (chopped)
2 Tbsp. parsley
2 Tbsp. black pepper
1 tsp. garlic
Dash of hot sauce
All purpose seasoning
Water

Option - Add a little milk or heavy cream
          Add corn

Combine ingredients in a large pot. Bring to boil, then simmer for 1 hour.

Quick tip - If your chowder is too thin, add powdered mashed potatoes until you get the desired consistency.

Serve in a bread bowl with oyster crackers.

VEGETARIAN CHILI

4 cans vegetarian chili
1 bell pepper (chopped)
½ cup onion (minced)
½ cup green onion (diced)
1 diced zucchini
½ cup corn
1 bunch cilantro (chopped)
Dash of cumin
¼ tsp. chili powder
Garlic powder (4 or 5 shakes)
½ cup salsa

Crock Pot - Cook all day on the low setting.

Pan - Bring to bubble then simmer for about 15 minutes.

Options -
Top with cheese
Serve in bread bowls
Serve with nachos or quesadillas

CHICKEN SOUP

Chicken (skinless, boneless)
Chicken giblets
2 tsp. apple cider vinegar
2 cans fat-free chicken broth
2 cups chopped celery
1 onion (chopped)
½ cup minced parsley
6 cloves garlic (or 3 Tbsp. garlic)
Dash of lemon
Water (to fill the pot)
Poultry seasoning
All purpose seasoning

Variations - Cilantro
              Rice
              Noodles

Crock Pot:
Add ingredients to crock pot. Cook on low until dinnertime.

Skim fat from soup. Serve with crackers or rolls.

To rush it:
Pour everything in a pot and cook it on the stove for about an hour.

If you want to make your soup the old-fashioned way:
Start with a whole chicken. Boil it for 15 minutes, then simmer for 1 hour.

Remove the chicken from your pot and tear the meat from the bones with a fork. *Watch your fingers, it will be hot.* Stir the broth with a strainer to remove any small bones.

Place the boneless, shredded chicken back in the pot. Add the other ingredients. Bring to boil, then simmer for another hour.

BOUILLABAISSE

3 cups celery (finely diced)
1 onion (diced)
1 Tbsp. garlic (crushed or 2 cloves)
4 cups clam juice
2 bay leaves
¼ cup parsley (diced)
3 filets any type of white fish
      (chopped in quarters)
water (or beer)

Add ingredients to large pot or crock pot. Add water or beer to rim of pot. Cook for 2 hours on stove or 6 hours in a crock pot.

2 tsp. lemon juice
Dash of saffron
1 cup dry white wine
2 cups chopped tomatoes
Shrimp (uncooked, de-veined, shelled)
Littleneck clams (live, cleaned thoroughly)
Scallops
Mussels
Lobster tails
Season (salt & pepper) to taste

Clean and rinse the shellfish and add to the pot.

Cover pot and bring to low-boil. (Add lobster about 5 minutes before serving.) Cook until clams open and shrimp turns pink. (10 to 15 minutes). *Shrimp gets rubbery when it's overcooked. Put it in last.*

Serve with sour dough bread and big mugs of broth on the side for dipping.

FRENCH ONION SOUP

4 cups sliced onions
2 tsp. flour
6 cups beef broth
1 cup swiss cheese (grated)
1 cup Parmesan cheese (grated)
Toasted french bread

Brown the onions in butter or low-fat cooking spray. Add flour and cook for another minute. Stir in broth and bring to boil. Reduce heat and simmer for 15 minutes.

Pour soup in oven-proof bowls. Add 2 slices of toasted bread to each bowl. Cover with equal parts of cheese. Broil until bubbly, but not burnt. It doesn't take long. I usually keep my eyes on it, so I don't forget what I'm doing.

DIANE'S FRENCH ONION SOUP

3 lg. onions, thinly sliced
¼ cup butter
3 cloves crushed garlic
Thyme to taste
4 to 5 cups water
1 lg. pkg. seaweed
8 slices crusty french bread
1 cup shredded Swiss cheese

Saute onions very slowly with garlic in butter for 30 minutes. Add water and seaweed. Bring to rapid boil for 5 minutes. Lower flame, cover and simmer for at least one hour.

Place bread in bowls and ladle soup over it. Cover with cheese. Broil until cheese browns.

IF YOU WANT REAL GUMBO GO PICK SOME UP ~ SEAFOOD SOUP

1 cup sweet corn
1 cup lima beans
2 cups stewed tomatoes (cut up)
½ cup chicken broth
1 cup medium shrimp (shelled and deveined)
1 cup cubed chicken breast (skinless, boneless)
1 cup okra (sliced)
½ cup onion (sliced)
1 cup bell pepper (chopped)
3 Tbsp. diced green chiles
3 Tbsp. crushed garlic
¼ tsp. allspice
¼tsp. cayenne
⅛ tsp. cumin
¼ tsp. black pepper
3 cups cooked brown rice

Spray pan with low-fat cooking spray. Add vegetables and broth and bring to rapid boil. Continue to cook for 3 minutes stirring occasionally.

Add seasonings and chicken. Reduce heat to med-high and saute for 5 more minutes.

Stir in rice and shrimp. Cook until ingredients are thoroughly hot and shrimp is pink.

Serve with thick sliced bread.

SPICED CIDER

Apple juice
6 whole cinnamon sticks
1 tsp. whole allspice
1 Tbsp. whole cloves

Fill a crock pot with apple juice. Add spices. Turn crock pot on. Display cups nicely next to crock pot.

SPLIT PEA SOUP

1 lb. yellow or green split peas	Rinse and drain split peas.
2 stalks celery (diced)	
2 quarts water	In a large soup kettle, combine
1 onion (diced)	ingredients. Bring to rapid boil.
2 carrots (sliced)	
2 Tsp. tarragon	Reduce heat and simmer for 3 to 4
¼ Tsp. nutmeg	hours. Stir occasionally.
¼ cup chopped parsley	
½ Tsp. white pepper	Serve with crusty bread.
Dash of salt	
1 Tbsp. apple cider vinegar	*Option*: Add 2 smoked ham hocks or
1 bay leaf	a meaty ham bone.

Tip from Dish: *Take my word for it. Don't use a pressure cooker for this one ~ unless you really **want** to re-paint the kitchen. It's incredible! One tiny, little half of a pea gets stuck in the nozzle of the pressure cooker and KABOOM! Splat! Plop, plop, plop. Months later, you're still burning peas every time you make toast.*

Flo: Months later?

RABBIT FOOD

RABBIT FOOD
Chewing is a great way to exercise!

CHINESE CHICKEN SALAD

1 small pkg won ton skins
4 to 6 chicken breasts (boneless, skinless)
1 to 2 heads lettuce
3 green onions
Cilantro
Slivered almonds (toasted)
Sesame seeds

Dressing:
1 Tbsp. toasted sesame seeds
½ cup vegetable oil
2 Tbsp. sesame oil
2 Tbsp. sugar
½ tsp. pepper
1 tsp. salt (optional)
4 Tbsp. rice vinegar

Cut the won ton skins into strips. Fry until a golden brown. Drain on a paper towel.

Roast or boil chicken and chop up. Break apart lettuce. Chop green onion including stem. Chop cilantro.

Combine salad ingredients, except won ton skins. Prepare dressing and mix well. Add dressing to salad and toss. Add the won ton skins and toss again. Serve.

Option: Add mandarin orange slices.

CUCUMBER SALAD

2 cucumbers (thinly sliced)
1 onion (thinly sliced)
¼ cup seasoned rice vinegar

Combine ingredients in a bowl. Cover and refrigerate 1 hour.

Option: Add cooked shrimp and diced chives

LILLIAN'S COLE SLAW

¾ cup sugar
1 lg. head of cabbage (sliced thin. Or use
        a couple of bags of shredded cabbage)
2 lg. red onions (sliced thin)

Stir sugar into cabbage, place ½ of the cabbage in a large bowl and add ½ of the onions. Then add the rest of the cabbage and onions. Set aside.

Dressing:
1 tsp. celery seed
1 tsp. sugar
1 tsp. dry mustard
1½ tsp. salt (optional)
1 cup apple cider vinegar
1 cup safflower oil

In a saucepan combine the 1st five ingredients (not the oil). Bring to a boil stirring occasionally. Stir in oil and bring back to boil. Pour boiling hot dressing over cabbage mixture. DO NOT STIR.

Cover and chill for 24 hours. Stir before serving.

Option: Add sliced cucumber to celery and onion mixture.
        Use less oil if you'd like.

CARROT APPLE CASSEROLE

Thinly sliced carrots
Thinly sliced apples
Sugar substitute
Cinnamon

Spray a pan with low fat cooking spray. Layer your carrots and apples. Add a dash of cinnamon and sugar substitute. Add a dab or two of butter. Bake at 350 until tender.

Great sweet side dish!

Option: If you don't like sugar substitutes, use honey instead. Drizzle just a little on top. You won't need much!

ROASTED SALAD

Fresh green beans
Corn
Avocado (cut into ¼" cubes)
Tomato (chopped)
Green onion (chopped)
Zucchini (sliced)
Yellow squash (sliced)
Cilantro or parsley (diced)
Roasted chicken breast or shrimp (cubed)
Lettuce (chopped)
Olive oil
Balsamic vinegar

Saute ingredients together in **½ tsp. olive oil** and **1 Tbsp. balsamic vinegar**.

Cook over high heat, stirring constantly for 2 to 3 minutes. Add all purpose seasoning and 2 cup of chopped lettuce. Toss and serve.

Option: Substitute your favorite Italian or Chinese style dressing for the oil and vinegar.

Tip from Flo: If you have the time, roast the ingredients in the oven for 5 minutes at 450 degrees before tossing the salad in. It adds a really nice flavor to the vegetables!

JACK'S RIZUTTO

Fresh spinach (washed thoroughly)
Rice (cooked)
Olives (diced)
Tomato (chopped)
Onion (chopped)
Artichoke hearts (packed in water, drained)
Eggplant (cubed)

Chop the vegetables and saute together. Add rice and cook for another 2 to 3 minutes.

Toss in balsamic, rice or apple cider vinegar. Sprinkle with all purpose seasoning and black pepper.

Option: Add a tad of olive oil or your favorite dressing.

CORI'S PEA SALAD

30 oz. defrosted peas
1 lb. bacon (chopped and cooked)
1 bunch green onions (chopped)
8 oz. sour cream
1 Tbsp. mayonnaise
Salt & pepper to taste

Mix together and refrigerate for 3 hours. Stir before serving.

CHOP 'TIL YOU DROP SALAD

Combine the following fresh ingredients:

1 cup corn (sliced from cob)
½ cup cilantro (minced)
2 or 3 tomatoes (chopped)
1 zucchini (cubed)
6 green onions (diced)
1 red cabbage (sliced)
1 head romaine lettuce (shredded)
1 cup spinach (torn)
¼ cup mushrooms (sliced)
½ cup fresh string beans (sliced at an angle)
½ cup peas (or pea pods, sliced at an angle)
¼ cup beets (grated)
½ cup carrots (grated)
½ cup broccoli (chopped)
½ cup red onion (minced)

Place the lettuce, spinach and red cabbage in a bowl and toss. Layer the other ingredients on top. Toss just before serving *(after your company sees how pretty it is!)*

Dressing ideas:
¼ cup balsamic vinegar, 1 tsp. crushed garlic, all purpose seasoning, pepper and just a tad of olive oil.

OR.

Seasoned rice vinegar and a dash of sesame oil.

SPINACH MASHED POTATOES

9 potatoes (cubed)
½ cup red onion (diced)
½ cup green onion (chopped)
2 cups fresh spinach (washed and drained)
2 tsp. crushed garlic
3 Tbsp. butter or yogurt
Parmesan cheese

Cook potatoes in large pot of water, uncovered. Bring to rapid boil. Reduce heat and cook for about 25 minutes until potatoes are soft. Drain.

Mix in garlic, butter or yogurt. Beat until smooth. Add onions and spinach. Stir and serve. Salt and pepper to taste. Sprinkle with Parmesan.

MOM'S LABOR-OF-LOVE SALAD MIX

Basic salad mix:
1 red bell pepper
3 zucchini
½ bunch of cilantro
3 to 6 green beans
Fresh corn (cut the kernels
       from 3 or 4 ears of corn)

Optional ingredients to vary flavor:
Red onion
Cucumber
Tomato
Carrot
Cooked chicken breast
Blue corn chips

Chop into pieces about the size of your "pinkie" fingernail (*your* nail doll, not the enamel one). Mix together in a bowl.

Note: The salad mix is fabulous in omelets!

LOW-CAL **1000** ISLAND SALAD

4 cups romaine lettuce
2 cups basic salad mix
1 cup cooked chicken breast

Toss (only as far as the bowl).

Add chicken breast and decorate with a few blue corn chips.

Dressing:
½ cup low-fat yogurt
½ cup low-cal Thousand Island dressing

This makes enough for several individual salads. Mix up a batch ahead of time and use it all week.

CHINESE CHICKEN SALAD

4 cups romaine lettuce
2 cup basic salad mix
4 green onions (diced)
1 cup chopped chicken breast (cooked, skinless).

Toss together. Add bottled dressing.

SANTA FE SALAD

2 cups basic salad mix
3 cups of corn
½ cup additional chopped cilantro
¼ cup green onions (diced)
¼ cup red onion (chopped)
1 cup shredded chicken (cooked)
Lettuce leaves

Mix thoroughly. Toss with a small amount of shredded chicken breast.

Lay lettuce leaves on a platter. Spoon salad mixture onto lettuce leaves and form into a mound.

Sprinkle more shredded chicken on top. Garnish with more chopped red bell pepper, cilantro and blue corn chips.

Serve with a salad dressing of your choice.

Option: Have your mom bring it.

NO KIDDING!
YOU WANT TO COOK BREAKFAST?

NO KIDDING!
YOU WANT TO COOK BREAKFAST?

VEGETABLE OMELETTE

The Snow White Way - After greeting your backyard bunnies and birds, pick fresh bell pepper, green onion, broccoli and tomato from your garden. Bring them into the cottage and place them on the counter beside the dazzling bouquet of flowers that you've just arranged. Wash and chop the vegetables, one by one.

Spray an omelet pan with no-fat cooking spray, then saute the colorful vegetables over medium heat for about a minute. Place the vegetables on the side plate you made on your pottery wheel until you're ready for them.

Beat 3 eggs and pour them into the pan. After the eggs start to bubble, flip gently, then add the braised vegetables.   Sprinkle with grated cheese. Cover the pan and cook until the cheese melts. Fold the omelet carefully onto a plate and garnish it with a lovely cluster of frosted red grapes.

Serve with the fresh, warm, cinnamon-raisin muffins that you made after drying the grapes from your vines.

The Pre-Fab Way - Take the lettuce out of last night's salad and toss the leftovers in a frying pan with some eggs and cheese. Cook over medium heat, scraping the bottom of the pan with a spatula once in awhile. Serve with bagels.

So it's not an omelet. You want an omelet? Go to Snow White's house.

MOM'S CINNAMON ROLLS

It wouldn't be Christmas morning without the smell of something wonderful, burning in the kitchen.

Any ready-made cinnamon rolls (with raisins)

Remove cellophane.
Wrap in foil.
Place in 425 degree oven.
Wait for the smoke alarm to go off.
Toss into trash can.

Tip from Flo: Keep a large container of baking soda or salt handy to put out those pesky fires.

BALTIC DELIGHT

Plain Yogurt
Fresh fruit
Bran muffin

Tip from Dish: Save any leftover yogurt for a moisturizing facial!

BLUEBERRY MUFFINS

1 pkg. blueberry muffin mix

Add in:
2 Tbsp. cinnamon
½ cup fresh or frozen blueberries
½ cup walnuts (chopped)

Follow directions on the package

Bake at 350 for 10 to 15 minutes or until golden brown.

ZUCCHINI PANCAKES & WAFFLES

For pancakes or waffles -
½ cup grated zucchini
1 Tbsp. cinnamon
½ tsp. vanilla

Use your standard mix. Leave out ¼ of the liquid. Add zucchini, cinnamon and vanilla.

Separate the egg whites from the yolks. Add the yolks to the pancake or waffle mix (*or leave them out entirely*.) Whip the egg whites until they form little peaks, then fold them into the mix, gently. Do not overmix. The batter should be slightly lumpy.

Option: Substitute warm jelly or honey for syrup or try a fresh fruit puree on top!

Tip from Flo: Make extra and freeze them in individual servings. Very handy during work week. Just toast them until warm. Serve as usual.

Cook normally until golden brown. Serve with warm maple syrup.

ZUCCHINI BREAD

3 eggs
1 cup oil
2 cups brown sugar
2 cups zucchini (grated)
2 tsp. vanilla

Mix together

Then add:
3 cups flour
1 tsp. baking soda
¼ tsp. baking powder
3 Tbsp. cinnamon
½ cup chopped walnuts

Pour into greased and floured baking pan. Bake at 325 for 75 minutes.

Option: Add raisins. You can substitute apple sauce for oil to make a fat-free bread.

TODD'S SCRAMBLED EGGS

One dozen eggs
1 bell pepper (chopped)
6 green onions (diced)
¼ cup diced green chiles
1 tomato (chopped)
6 mushrooms (sliced)
½ cup onion (chopped)
1 zucchini (chopped)
½ cup salsa
All purpose seasoning
Last night's leftover steak (cubed)

Saute vegetables and steak over medium heat. Scramble eggs and pour into pan stirring occasionally.

Roll in warm tortillas or serve with hot biscuits and gravy.

Option: Add grated cheese

CINNAMON FRENCH TOAST

Eggs
1 tsp. vanilla
2 Tbsp. cinnamon
Sliced bread

Whip together. Drop bread in bowl and soak for 1 minute on each side.

Saute in butter or margarine for about 2 minutes over medium heat.

Sprinkle with more cinnamon while cooking. Turn and cook the other side until golden brown.

Serve with hot maple syrup and powdered sugar.

Option: Add a little milk to the egg mixture.

Tip from Flo: Freeze the rest to use later. Just toast and serve.

BREAKFAST BURRITOS

6 eggs
Refried or vegetarian beans
Diced green chiles
2 green onions (chopped)
1 tomato (diced)
Salsa
Flour tortillas

Saute onions and tomato over medium heat for about a minute. Scramble eggs and pour in pan. Add green chiles and salsa. Cook until eggs are fluffy, stirring occasionally.

Heat beans until bubbly. Spread beans on tortillas. Add scrambled eggs and roll up.

(I like to heat the beans after they're rolled inside the burrito by tossing the whole mess in the microwave and nuking for 2 minutes.)

Option: Add cheese.

Tip from Flo: This dish tastes better when the beans are cooked the old-fashioned way, on the stove. You can add your cheese to the beans while cooking them. Spoon the cooked bean mixture onto your tortillas right before the eggs are done. Serve your burritos nice and hot!

FRESH HOT MUFFINS

1 pkg. of your favorite muffin mix
1 Tbsp. cinnamon
1 cup fresh or frozen fruit (or raisins)
1 cup chopped walnuts

This recipe is great with raisins, diced apples and extra cinnamon in a bran muffin mix! Also delicious is banana in a basic mix with ½ tsp. nutmeg instead of cinnamon. Other fruit ideas: Fresh berries, dried cranberries, dried or fresh chopped apricots or cherries.

Follow the directions on the packaged muffin mix.

Stir in spice, fruit and walnuts. Do not overmix. Spoon mixture into muffin or baking pan. Bake at 350 for 15 to 25 minutes, until done.

Place fresh muffins in a basket lined with a linen napkin. Serve hot!

NANA'S PUMPKIN BREAD

1 ½ cups sugar
½ Tsp. baking powder
1 Tsp. baking soda
Dash of salt
1 Tbsp. cinnamon
1 Tbsp. nutmeg
1 Tbsp. cloves
1 ½ cups flour
1 cup oil
½ cup water
1 cup pumpkin
2 eggs
½ cup chopped nuts
½ cup raisins or dates, if desired

Do not sift dry ingredients. Mix all together in order given.

Grease and flour one large bread pan or two small loaf pans, lightly. Pour mixture into pan(s) and bake at 325 for 1 ½ hours.

When done, remove from oven and let it stand for 5 or 6 minutes. Slip a knife between the edge of the bread and the edge of the pan. Gently glide the knife around the edges, loosening the bread.

Place a serving plate upside down on top of the pan. Turn the pan upside down and the bread should fall out on plate.

Serve plain, with softened butter or whipped cream cheese.

Tip from Flo: Check doneness by poking a toothpick or knife into center of bread. If it comes out clean, your bread is done. If a little dough clings to it, put it back in the oven and bake for a few more minutes. Let the bread rest in the pan for 10 minutes before cutting.

Tip from Dish: If the pumpkin bread doesn't come out, tap gently on the bottom of the pan. If it still doesn't come out, give it a few hard whacks until it falls onto the plate. Now, if it's still stuck, check it to make sure it's edible. Smell it to make sure it's not too burnt. If it's OK, slice it in the pan and let your guests serve themselves ~ Or, turn it into dessert! Scoop the pumpkin bread out of the pan with a large spoon. Cover it all over with gobs of whipped cream and refrigerate for one hour. See? Cooking can be fun!

SMOOTHIES

SMOOTHIES

Use organic produce and filtered water whenever available.

BASIC SMOOTHIE

1 large scoop protein powder
1 banana
1 cup fruit
1 cup liquid
1 cup crushed ice (or ½ cup crushed ice and 1 cup nonfat frozen yogurt)

Dairy -

CHOCOLATE

Chocolate-flavored protein powder, nonfat frozen yogurt, nonfat milk, crushed ice, banana.

BERRY DELIGHT

Plain protein powder, nonfat frozen yogurt or sorbet, frozen blackberries, frozen boysenberries, banana, 1/4 cup boysenberry juice, crushed ice.

TROPICAL BREEZE

Plain protein powder, nonfat frozen yogurt, banana, pineapple juice, pineapple-coconut juice, crushed ice.

STRAWBERRY-BANANA

Plain protein powder, nonfat frozen yogurt, strawberries, a banana, apple juice, crushed ice.

CARROT SHAKE

Plain protein powder, nonfat frozen yogurt, fresh carrot juice, crushed ice.

PASSION PEACH

Plain protein powder, sliced peaches, nonfat frozen yogurt, peach nectar, crushed ice.

ORANGE FREEZE

Plain protein powder, frozen orange juice, nonfat frozen yogurt, 1 tsp. whey powder, crushed ice.

Non-Dairy -

Omit the yogurt and milk from the dairy versions. Substitute with sorbet if you'd like. Skip the sorbet and add extra fruit, juice and ice for a lower-cal version.

TROPICAL COCKTAIL
Plain protein powder, banana, papaya, pineapple, mango, pineapple coconut juice, ice.

AMERICAN FLAG
Plain protein powder, strawberries, blueberries, banana, apple juice, ice.

BERRY-RAMA
Plain protein powder, blackberries, boysenberries, strawberries, raspberries, banana, boysenberry-apple juice, ice.

Tip from Flo: *Dice fruit before blending for easier mixing.*

Optional additions:
Powdered lecithin
Whey powder (a more easily digestible dairy product)
Nonfat plain yogurt
Calcium powder
Vitamin C powder
Honey
Spirulina
Liver powder
Brewer's yeast

Don't look at me! I don't want it.

Options -
Cut the juice with half water for fewer calories.
Apple juice makes a good base juice for most smoothies. Try the unfiltered type.
Also - you can leave out the banana if you'd like.

Tip from Dish: *The smoothies are much better when you leave the liver powder and brewer's yeast out of the recipe. If you want to take them, try the tablet form. Unless, of course, you enjoy the taste of dried, fermented, spicy dirt in your shakes. Don't stand on your head after drinking them, either.*

UDDER DECADENCE

UDDER DECADENCE

Dairy, Desserts and Devilish Dips
This section's bad!

CRAB DIP

Sourdough bread round
French bread - (have them slice
                it for you at the store)
1 cup sour cream
4 green onions (chopped)
2 cups grated cheddar cheese
8 oz. cream cheese
12 oz. crab meat (drained)
Hot sauce
Seasoning

Mix sour cream, cream cheese, crab meat, cheese and green onions together in a bowl. Spread on your thighs...no, just kidding. Add seasoning and hot sauce.

Cut a hole in the top of the bread round and scoop out the insides to make a bowl. Save the scooped out bread for dipping. Save the top for decoration. Spoon the crab mixture into the bread bowl and wrap in heavy foil. Bake at 350 for 1 hour.

Add a spreading knife and serve with bread and crackers.

CREAMED CORN

8 oz. whipping cream
8 oz. half & half
1 tsp. salt (optional)
6 tsp. sugar
1 pinch pepper

Add:
20 oz. frozen corn (partially defrosted)
2 Tbsp. butter
2 Tbsp. flour

Warm ingredients in a saucepan.

Add corn to cream mixture. Heat to a boil, then simmer for 5 minutes. Melt butter in a separate pan. Mix butter and flour together, then add to corn mixture. Stir and serve.

NACHOS

Tortilla chips
Grated cheddar cheese (Lots)
Vegetarian chili (2 cans)
½ cup chopped cilantro
1 tsp. garlic powder
½ Tbsp. all purpose seasoning
Salsa

Place chips in a glass pan. Smother the tortilla chips with gobs of grated cheese. Microwave on high for 3 or 4 minutes until cheese is melted but *not* bubbly. (*Bubbling makes the cheese hard.*)

In a saucepan, combine vegetarian chili, cilantro and spices. Bring to boil, stirring frequently.

Serve nachos with chili dip on the side. Garnish with salsa, guacamole and a tad of cilantro.

Preparation time: About 10 minutes.

"NO GUILT ALLOWED" CHILI CHEESE DIP
Not much in this sucker is good for you, so forget about it and enjoy!

1 lg. pkg. *processed* cheese
8 oz. pkg. regular cream cheese
2 cans hot chili without beans

Turn your crock pot on low. Add ingredients, cover and cook until melted.

Serve over tortilla chips with a side of salsa.

Option: Jalapeno peppers (sliced)

Tip from Flo: *This stuff really disappears at parties! You'll run out early. For a large party, have another crock pot going in the kitchen to replace the empty one.*

Tip from Dish: *It may take you a day or two to get back to normal after eating this stuff. It's so good, you'll want to eat a lot! I'm not sure whether it's the gas or the bloating that gets me the day after, but I usually hide until it goes away.*

DECADENT SPINACH MASHED POTATOES

9 potatoes
4 Tbsp. butter or margarine
½ tsp. garlic
3 Tbsp. milk
10 oz. pkg. frozen chopped spinach
             (thawed and well-drained)
8 oz. pkg. cream cheese (cut up)
½ cup diced artichoke hearts
Salt & pepper to taste
Parmesan cheese

Cut up the potatoes (peel them if you'd like). Add them to a large pot of water (uncovered). Bring to boil then reduce heat and cook until soft. Drain.

Add cream cheese, butter and garlic. Beat potatoes until smooth. Gradually add just enough milk to make them fluffy. Mix in spinach and artichoke hearts. Salt and pepper to taste.

Spoon mixture into baking dish. Cover and bake for about 30 minutes at 325 until hot.

Remove from oven and sprinkle with Parmesan cheese.

BEEF ENCHILADAS

1 lb. ground beef
1 onion (chopped)

Diced olives
Grated cheddar cheese
Enchilada sauce
Tortillas

Garnish with diced tomatoes, cilantro and salsa!

Cook meat and onion together. Drain oil.

Heat sauce, add water if necessary. Warm tortilla in sauce then lay in a baking dish. Add 1 Tbsp. beef, 1 Tbsp. olives and 2 Tbsp. cheese to tortilla and roll up. Repeat. Top with more enchilada sauce. Sprinkle with more cheese.

Bake at 350 for 30 to 45 minutes. Or nuke on high for 10.

STELLA'S CARROT CAKE

2 cups flour
2 cups sugar
¼ tsp. baking powder
1 tsp. baking soda
1 tsp. nutmeg
1 tsp. cloves
1 Tbsp. cinnamon
4 eggs (beaten)
1½ cups vegetable oil
2 cups grated carrots
1 cup chopped walnuts
Icing:
8 oz. pkg. cream cheese (softened)
½ cup butter or margarine
1 tsp. vanilla
1 lb. pkg. powdered sugar

Sift together dry ingredients. Blend eggs and oil together until creamy. Add dry ingredients and carrots to egg mixture.

Pour into greased and floured cake pans. Bake at 350 for 1 hour.

Cream together the cream cheese and butter. Add vanilla and powdered sugar. Beat until smooth. Spread on cooled cake. Garnish with chopped walnuts.

Ahhh!
Turn it Off!
Turn it Off!

Tip from Dish ~ Keep your head away from the mixing bowl.

THE VERY BEST RUM CAKE EVER!

1 or 2 quarts of fine rum
1 cup butter
1 tsp. sugar
1 very large eggs
1 cup dried up fruit
1 tsp. soda
Some baking powder
Lemon juice
Brown sugar
Nuts

Before you start, sample the rum to make sure it is of the finest quality. Good, isn't it? Now go ahead. Select a large mixing bowl, measuring cup, etc. Now, check the rum again -- it must be of the highest quality. The best way to check it is to pur one level cup of rum into a glass and drink it as fast as you can. Repeat.

With an electric mixer, beat 1 cup butter in a large fluffy bowl. Add one teaspoon of thugar and beat again. Meanwhile, make sure the rum is of excellent quality -- try another cup. Open 2nd quart of rum if necessary. Add 2 arge leggs, 2 cups of fried druit and beat till high. If druit gets stuck in the beaters, just eject them and bang them on the counter until the druit flies out. Sample the rum again checking for tonacisticity.

Nex, sift 3 cups of pepper or salt (it really doesn't matter). Test the rum again and sift ½ pint of jemon luice. Fold in chopped butter and whipped nuts. Add some brown thugar or whatever color you can find.

Grease oven and turn cake pan to 350 gredees. Now pour the whole mess into the oven, check the rum again...and bo to ged!

LEMON·FROSTED CRESCENT ROLLS

1 or 2 pkgs. crescent dough

Filling:
8 oz. cream cheese
¼ cup sugar
1½ tsp. vanilla

Mix filling ingredients together. Spread on dough roll up. Shape into crescents. Bake as per the instructions on the crescent roll package.

Frosting:
2 cups powdered sugar
⅓ cup lemon juice

Mix together. Spread over hot, fresh from the oven crescent rolls. Serve immediately.

WOW! THESE·ARE·SOOO·GOOD! BARS
(That's what everybody says the first time they bite into these.)

½ cup butter or margarine
1½ cup crushed graham cracker
14 oz. can sweetened condensed milk
6 oz. pkg. semi-sweet chocolate chips
3½ oz. can flaked coconut
1 cup chopped nuts

Preheat oven to 350. In a 13" x 9" pan, melt the butter. Sprinkle graham cracker over melted butter. Pour milk evenly in pan.

In a separate bowl, mix coconut, chips and nuts. Spread mixture inside pan and pat down.

Bake for 20 to 35 minutes. Cool completely. Inhale. Cut leftovers into squares. Usually makes 24 bars.

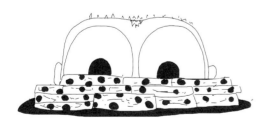

CHEESECAKE

Who has time to make a cheesecake? Buy one from the bakery. If it's not pretty enough, add a topping:

Ideas:

Shaved white chocolate and whipped cream - Squirt a whipped cream design on your cheesecake. "Shave" a bar of white chocolate with a knife to make 1" curls and sprinkle them over the whipped cream.

Flavored whipped cream - Add a Tbsp. of your favorite flavoring while mixing whipping cream in your blender. (chocolate, almond, mocha, rum, Kahlua)

Strawberry - Slice 1 package of strawberries, add 2 Tbsp. honey, stir together. Spoon on to cheesecake.

Blueberry - Thaw frozen blueberries. Add 2 Tbsp. honey, mix together. Spoon over cheesecake.

Cherry - Canned cherry pie filling. Spoon onto cheesecake. Garnish with whipped cream. *Actually any type of canned pie filling works well!*

Mix it up - Fresh raspberries, blueberries, blackberries and sliced kiwi.

LEMON WHIPPERSNAPS
Oh my goodness!

1 pkg. lemon cake mix
2 cups whipped topping
1 egg
Powdered sugar

Mix together. Spoon dollops 1 ½" apart on a greased cookie sheet.

Bake at 350 for about 10 minutes or until golden. Drop hot cookies gently into powdered sugar. Cool.

FUDGE BROWNIE SUNDAES

Brownies
Ice cream or non-fat frozen yogurt
Hot fudge topping
Whipped cream
Chopped nuts

Option - Use mint chip ice cream!

Heat fudge topping in microwave for about a minute.

Crumble the brownies. (I got this idea one evening, after dropping the pan on the floor.)
Layer parfait glasses with brownies, hot fudge and ice cream. Top with whipped cream and nuts.

You can always exercise it off later!

EASY ALMOND ROCA

1 cup butter (room temp.)
1 cup sugar
3½ oz. blanched slivered almonds
1 lg. chocolate bar
1 cup minced pecans or walnuts

Start with a cold frying pan or electric skillet and a wooden spoon. Place butter and sugar in skillet and cook on high, stirring constantly, for 3 minutes.

Add the almonds and reduce heat to 320 for another 3 minutes. Stir constantly — sugar burns easily. Increase heat to high again and stir for another 2 to 3 minutes. Cook until mixture turns a coffee and cream color.

Remove from heat and quickly pour into an ungreased 13" x 9" pan. Spread evenly. Break up chocolate bar and place on top. As it melts, spread it evenly. Sprinkle nuts on top and press into chocolate. Cool completely, then break into pieces.

Tip from Flo: You'll have to work very fast. Have everything ready and measured before you begin. Have your ungreased 13" x 9" pan near you. **Be very careful!** This hot mixture can cause severe burns! Keep the kids and pets out of the kitchen while you're making it.

PHEFFERNEUSE

I bake these once a year - holiday season. No matter how much I make, I always run out.

2 cups flour
1 cup butter or margarine
6 Tbsp. sugar
1 cup walnuts
½ Tsp. vanilla
1 pkg. powdered sugar

Sift the flour into a bowl. Add butter and granulated sugar. Cut the butter into the flour using two knives.

Then, mix the ingredients together using your hands. Batter will be "grainy" (tiny clumps of flour and butter).

Now - ***Depending on the type of day you've had*** *-* Chop the nuts into fine even pieces, or SMASH the bag with a mallet as hard as you can, then spoon the mush into your bowl.

Pound!
Kerplop!
Whack!

Roll the dough into ½ inch balls and place on an ungreased cookie sheet. *Tip -* Save your nails. Have the kids roll them into little balls. If you don't have kids, borrow some.

Bake at 350 for about 10 minutes or until golden.

Whack! WHACK!
WHACK! WHACK!
WHACK! KERPOW!!!
WHACK! WHACK!
WHACK!!

Remove from oven. Using a spatula, gently place hot cookies in a bowl of powdered sugar. Roll each cookie lightly in powdered sugar.

Watch them! They'll disappear before your eyes!

Well, I don't have to ask how your day was.

GRACE'S ALMOND SUGAR COOKIES

1 cup butter
1 cup sugar
1 cup powdered sugar

Cream together until fluffy.

Add:
1 cup oil
2 eggs

Blend with sugar mixture until creamy.

Sift into fluffy, creamy mixture:
4½ cups flour
1 tsp. cream of tartar
1 tsp. baking soda
1½ tsp. almond extract

Stir gently with fork until dry ingredients are mixed in. Do not over mix.

Chill for 1 hour. Roll into balls and press with fork. Bake at 350 for 12 minutes. Remove from oven and dip in sugar. Yummy.

NANA'S APPLE CRISP

6 apples
½ cup sugar

Slice apples and lay in greased baking dish. Sprinkle sugar on top.

Topping:
½ cup melted butter
½ cup brown sugar
¾ cup flour
½ cup raisins

Mix together brown sugar, butter, raisins and flour. Sprinkle on top of apples. Bake at 325 for 30 minutes.

Serve hot over vanilla ice cream.

Option: Add 1 Tbsp. cinnamon to apples.

JEWEL COOKIES

½ cup butter or margarine
¼ cup brown sugar
1 egg yolk
1 tsp. vanilla
1 cup flour

Topping:
1 egg white
1 cup diced walnuts or pecans
Strawberry jelly

*Option: Use festive colors of jelly
for different holidays and occasions!*

Mix together with a fork. (For a flakier cookie, do not over mix.) Refrigerate for 1 hour.

Remove cookie dough from fridge and roll into 1" balls. Dip each one in egg yolk then roll in diced nuts.

Place cookie balls on lightly greased cookie sheet. Press a blip in the center of each cookie with your finger.

Bake at 375 for about 8 minutes, until done. Spoon a dollop of jelly into each cookie hole and arrange on a plate.

AUNT DOT'S PEANUT BUTTER COOKIES

1 cup peanut butter
½ cup butter
½ cup sugar
½ cup brown sugar
1 tsp. vanilla
1 egg
1½ cups flour (sifted)
¾ tsp. baking soda
½ tsp. baking powder
Dash of salt

Cream peanut butter and butter. Add sugars. Add vanilla and egg. Beat well.

Sift dry ingredients together and add to creamed mixture. Stir. Add chocolate chips or chopped nuts, if desired.

Form into little round balls. Dip fork in water then press top of each cookie ball forming plaid pattern. Bake at 375 for 8-10 minutes until golden brown.

MOM'S LEMON CAKE

1 pkg. lemon cake mix
1 pkg. instant vanilla or lemon pudding
4 eggs
¾ cup oil
½ cup lemon juice

Beat for five minutes on medium speed (you'll need a mixer for this one). Pour into sprayed and floured cake or molding pan. Bake at 350 for 35 to 45 minutes.

Frosting:
1 pkg. powdered sugar
½ cup butter
1 tsp. vanilla
¼ cup grated lemon rind
Juice from one lemon

Beat together on medium speed until blended. Spread on cooled cake.

MOM'S PARTY CAKE

1 pkg. yellow cake mix
1 pkg. instant vanilla pudding
4 eggs
¾ cup oil
¾ cup dry sherry
1 tsp. nutmeg

Beat for five minutes on medium speed. Pour into greased and floured 10 inch tube pan or bundt cake pan.

Bake at 350 for 45 minutes. Serve without frosting.

DISH'S LEMON CAKE

Dial the bakery. Order it! Extra lemon.

DEVILISH DOUBLE-RICH CHOCOLATE CAKE

1 pkg. chocolate cake mix
Egg (see pkg. mix)
Oil (see pkg. mix)
Water (see pkg. mix)
1 small pkg. chocolate chips
2 or 3 Tbsp. sour cream

Follow directions on package, but reduce the water by 2 or 3 Tbsp. Add in sour cream and beat as directed on box. Stir in chocolate chips. Bake as directed on cake mix package.

Frosting:
1 pkg. powdered sugar
½ cup butter or margarine
1 tsp. vanilla
¼ cup sour cream
Milk
Chocolate powder

Beat together until creamy. Add chocolate powder to taste. Add milk until it reaches desired consistency. Spread on cooled cake.

EASY BITE-SIZE DESSERTS

1 pkg. frozen puff pastry sheets (thawed)

Filling options:
Chocolate chips
Mincemeat
Canned pie filling

On a lightly floured surface, cut puff pastry dough into squares. Add about 2 Tbsp. filling in the center of each square.

Lift the corners of the square and twist together.

Place on an ungreased cookie sheet and bake at 400 for about 10 minutes until the shells are golden brown. Sprinkle with powdered sugar if desired.

CULINARY DELIGHT

1 Sunday paper
1 pair fuzzy slippers
1 beverage

Read the paper leisurely, clipping out double coupons as you go.

Later, take a pleasant drive toward the supermarket. Pass it by, you can shop later. Head for your favorite, cozy restaurant. Order a fabulous meal. Eat!

On your way home, stop at the market. Now browse through culinary heaven relaxed with a full tummy and a wonderful sense of well being. Take an exciting walk down the frozen food aisle and remind yourself just how much time you'll save cooking the Pre-Fab way!

Pick up packaged foods, read labels and plan your dining experiences for the week.

Take a few minutes to visit the cappuccino bar. *(This is Flo's favorite.)* Organize your coupons for a speedy check-out.

Then, drive home, unpack your groceries and relax by the fire with a huge cup of tea and one of those saucy novels.

PUZZLE CAKE

You're puzzled whether to eat it or toss it!

**4 prepared loaf pan size cakes
            (any type will do)**
Whipped topping
Powdered sugar

Slice your cake into chunks or layers.

Mix ½ cup powdered sugar into the whipped topping. Spread topping on layers. Repeat until you have your desired shape. Smooth the rest of the topping on the cake and make little swirls with a spoon.

We got this recipe from an accident in the kitchen.
Two cake layers crumbled out of their pans and fell on the counter. With dinner in 5 minutes, we had to work fast. "Glueing" the cake together with whipped cream (and powdered sugar for stiffness), we made an igloo. Our families thought it was very creative...Hah! They were lucky the cake didn't fall on the floor.

CAPPUCCINO BROWNIES

Packaged brownie mix (without nuts)
Read the package for the ingredients and oven setting.

You'll also need:
3 Tbsp. instant coffee
1 extra egg
¼ cup flour

Mix eggs, coffee and water together before adding them to the mix. Add egg mixture to packaged mix and stir in other items the brownie mix calls for. Spread into greased pan.

Snazzy Topping:
8 oz pkg. cream cheese
⅓ cup sugar
1 egg
2 Tbsp. flour
1½ tsp. cinnamon

Mix together. Spoon over brownie batter and swirl with a knife. Bake for 40 minutes.

Cool completely. Cut into squares. Try to save some for other family members.

HOT COCOA

Instant cocoa
Water
Whipped cream
Dash of cinnamon or cocoa

Pour instant cocoa mix into cup. Boil water and add to cup. Top with whipped cream. Sprinkle cinnamon or cocoa on top.

OR-

Mini-marshmallows
Instant cocoa
Water

Fill a cup half way up with mini-marshmallows. Pour instant cocoa mix into cup. Add boiling water. Stir.

Serve with big cookies, fuzzy slippers and a fun board game.

EASY COBBLER

2 cans pie filling
1 yellow cake mix
2 eggs
⅓ cup water
¼ cup melted butter

Spray a baking dish with low fat cooking spray. Dump in pie filling. Mix cake mix, eggs, water together. Spoon over fruit filling.

Drizzle melted butter and topping.

Bake at 350 for 45 minutes. Serve warm.

Topping options:
Cinnamon & sugar - for apple filling
Coconut & nuts - for cherry filling
Flour, hard butter, cinnamon and brown sugar -for French apple topping.

Option: Substitute frozen pie crust for cake mix. Thaw crust. Cut into strips. Arrange on top of pie filling. Add butter and topping. Bake.

EASIER COBBLER

2 cans pie filling
1 pre-made frozen pie crust

Thaw pie crust. Pour pie filling into greased baking dish. Break or slice pie crust into whatever shapes you desire and lay on top of pie filling.

Serve with vanilla ice cream or yogurt!

Bake until pie crust turns light brown.

BECKY'S LACE COOKIES

1 cup butter or margarine (softened)
1 cup brown sugar
1 cup sugar

Beat until smooth.

Then add:
1 egg
1 tsp. vanilla
1 tsp. baking soda
1 tsp. baking powder
1 tsp. salt (optional)
1 cup flour

Mix together

Then add:
1 cup coconut
2 cups old fashioned oatmeal
1 cup semi-sweet chocolate chips

Mix together and spoon onto cookie sheet.

Bake at 350 for 8 - 10 minutes until golden brown. Do not burn.

Cool slightly and move cookies to cooling rack.

KITCHEN SECRETS

KITCHEN SECRETS

Make your home smell like you cooked all day while you unpack dinner and hide the containers before company arrives.

APPLE PIE SMELL

1 apple
2 Tbsp. cinnamon
¼ cup water

Set oven to 350. Slice one apple into quarters, place in pie pan. Add water, sprinkle cinnamon on top. Bake until company comes.

Not enough time?

Add same ingredients to saucepan. Blaze that sucker on high until it boils. Reduce heat to simmer. Take off stove and hide the pan before your guests arrive.

GARLIC & ONIONS

The scent of garlic and onions always makes people think something wonderful is cooking. The fastest way to do this is in a frying pan.

3 cloves garlic
     (or 3 Tbsp. crushed garlic from the jar)
1 onion (sliced in chunks)
3 Tbsp. margarine
     (since you're not going to eat it, pile on the fat. It will smell better)

Cook uncovered over medium heat for 5 minutes.

Option: Substitute low cal cooking spray for margarine and throw in a cut-up chicken. Sprinkle with poultry seasoning, squeeze half a lemon over it and cover. Simmer for 30 min. This one you can eat!

AIR FRESHENER

Great for getting rid of cooked fish odors! Place a **lemon** in the oven and bake for 15 minutes at 350° with the oven door open. (If you're in a rush, turn it on high, but watch it. The smell of burnt lemon isn't much better than old fish.

HOW TO GET RID OF UNWANTED GUESTS

Surprise! Surprise! You have company! You had other plans, but now you have company! Don't sweat it, doll. Here are three ways to get rid of them without having to be rude:

Ah ~ The Smell Of It

Offer them coffee and go into the kitchen. Get out one large pot and fill it with about 4 inches of water. Chop a cabbage into quarters and throw it in the pot. Add 1 cup of vinegar. Bring to a boil leaving the pot uncovered. Sit down and chat for a moment. The aroma of boiling cabbage is quite an unusual one. Wait until its pungence permeates the room then invite your friends to stay for dinner. You'd better get their coats. They'll be running for the door.

What's That On Your Leg?

Ask your surprise guests to come in, but to watch where they step. Tell them your son just spilled his flea circus on the carpet. Get out the vacuum cleaner and say, "How nice of you to stop by!" If they're still there when you're finished vacuuming, ask them "You're not allergic to bug spray are you?" Your guests should be leaving now. If they don't get the hint, try the next suggestion.

The Tired Act

Invite your friends to have a seat and ask them how they've been. As they tell you, start to nod off. Don't snore though, you'll start laughing and give it away. Pretend you're really tired and you're trying to keep your eyes open. Let your head sink suddenly then jerk it back up. Open your eyes really wide and ask another question. Blink a lot. They'll either get the hint and leave or think your hairdo's too heavy.

Getting Really Dense People to Leave

If none of the above suggestions worked, you can try this last one. I use it only as a last resort. Stick out your chin, force a smile so wide it makes the skin bunch up around your ears, bug your eyes out really big and growl at them without letting them answer back, "How are you? I'm fine. I always look this way this time of the month. PMS. Do you have chocolate? Leave now if you want to live. Run! Run!" You probably won't hear from them for quite awhile. Later, if you see men in white coats walking up your driveway, hide and lock the door.

New ideas may flow in from unexpected places. Some may even be good.

FLO'S CORNER

FLO'S CORNER
Creative ways to slice and dice

How to make vegetable flowers

You can use radishes, celery, green onions and carrots to make attractive garnishes.

Take a 2-3 inch long piece of vegetable (or a radish). Cut a checkerboard pattern in one end of the vegetable, lengthwise, about one third of the length. Place the cut vegetables in a bowl of ice water for about 10 minutes, then use as a garnish.

You can make another type of "flower" by cutting 5 or 6 thin V-shaped grooves into a vegetable.

After grooves are made, slice the vegetable into thin slices.

In most cases, you will have something that resembles a flower. Radishes, carrots, cucumber, yellow squash, zucchini, mushrooms and eggplant work well for this version.

On larger "flowers" you can use a small round cookie cutter to cut out centers. Mix and match your "flowers" and centers. (Carrot center on cucumber flower, etc.) You can also use fruit.

Leaves

Long thin green onions or cilantro pieces make fabulous leaves.

Curls

Use a peeler to cut long thin strips. They should naturally curl up.
Chill in ice water until you're ready to serve.

Shapes

You can use cookie cutters to make shapes from sliced fruit and vegetables.
Let the kids have fun with this one!

Dip bowls

Create your own bowls for cold party dip. Good bowl veggies: Tight red or green cabbage, bell peppers (any color), jicama, tomatoes. Place them on a platter lined with lettuce leaves.

Cabbage -   Use the core as the bottom. Slice a little off the top then use a bent grapefruit knife to cut out the bowl. (Don't go too deep.) Fill your bowl with dip.

Jicama -   Same as cabbage. This is a little more difficult to make.

Bell pepper - Choose peppers with even bottom and wide round shapes. Pick a pepper that will stand up. Cut out core and clean out seeds. Rinse, dry and fill with dip.

Tomato -   Tomatoes are great as individual dip bowls. With the stem as the top, cut the top off and scoop a bowl shape in the tomato. Fill with dip or tuna salad.

Artichokes - Cook the artichokes until tender. Carefully remove the center leaves making sure to leave the base and surrounding leaves in tact. Arrange the leaves around the artichoke on an attractive platter. Scoop out the purple choke or fuzzy stuff above the artichoke heart and discard. Fill the center of the artichoke with dip. When the dip is gone, eat the heart of your bowl!

Lemon twists

Slice a lemon into thin wheels. You can use them as is, or cut them in half and twist. If ou'd like, you can use the peels to snazz up water glasses. Cut the lemon peel into 1/4" wide, 1½ inch long strips. Twist them over the water glass to release the flavor. Then drop in.

Pear bunnies

Great fun at spring and birthday parties!

Pear halves
Red grapes
Raisins
Carrots
Cottage cheese
Orange slices
Whipped cream

Use a pear half for the bunny bodies. Cut the grapes in half and use them for eyes. Use the raisins for the noses. Slice the carrots diagonally into 1 inch slivers and use them for ears. Lay a lettuce leaf on a plate. Add a mound of cottage cheese. Place the bunnies on the mound of cottage cheese. Squirt a tad of whipped cream for the tail. Garnish with orange slices.

Orange boats

Cut an orange in half. Scoop out the insides and fill it up with chopped fruit. Cut a thin slice from the other half of the orange and stick a toothpick through it. Stick the toothpick in the center of the orange boat to make a sail. Cut a tiny thin piece of lemon and poke a toothpick through it. Stick the toothpick through the top of the "orange-sail" to make a flag. Serve on a lettuce leaf and garnish with a sprig of mint.

Fruit bowls

Many types of fruit make marvelous bowls. Melons, apples, oranges or any other round shaped fruit will do nicely. Cut an alternating V-shaped pattern in the middle of the fruit. Go all the way around until it comes apart. Scoop the insides out and fill with yogurt or fresh fruit. Go crazy and cut your fruit into a basket shape! Or ~ Make your fruit resemble a fish or a car by cutting accents into the sides and adding "fins" or "wheels". Garnish with those cute little umbrellas or plastic pink flamingos.

COOKING WITH HERBS
Herbs are best when fresh.

Basil - There are many types of fresh basil. The green, standard leaf basil that you get from the grocery store is the sweetest. Use it in Italian cuisine. Basil flowers are edible, pretty and quite spicy. Pick off flower pods and sprinkle on your favorite pasta! Tip for easy basil strips - Pull leaves off stems and stack them. Roll the leaves up into a tube shape, then cut.

Opal Basil - A beautiful, purple basil that is a bit stronger and spicier than the green type. Add it to bottled vinegar for use on salads and other dishes.

Chives - They have the cutest little purple flowers in the spring! Chives add a bit of zing to baked potatoes, omelets and salads. You can also eat the flowers. Cut them up and use sparingly, as they have a stronger flavor than the leaves.

Dill - Fabulous on fish! Dice and add tomato for artichoke dip!

Garlic - We love garlic! It's wonderful in many dishes and fabulous in the garden. I grow it near my roses to help keep the aphids away. It has also been said to keep away colds. (That's because people don't come near you after you eat a lot of it.)

Oregano - The familiar herb in Italian sauces, oregano has a hearty, robust flavor. It's great on meats and in soups, too.

Mint - Delicious in iced tea! Nice garnish too.

Poultry Seasoning - Use in chicken dishes. Just like Mom used to make before she taught you how to cook!

Rosemary - Wonderful in bottled vinegars. Fabulous on lamb or chicken. Remove leaves and save stems. You can use the wood-like stems as skewers for chicken shish kabobs!

Sage - Used quite often in holiday meals. Sage has a slightly bitter, musty taste. Use it on poultry and in stuffing.

Thyme - Thyme is good on almost anything. It adds a light minty, almost lemony flavor to fish, chicken and vegetables.

Tarragon - Often used in bouquet gari, tarragon has a light, licorice taste. Flavor sauces, meats, vinegar and fish with tarragon.

FRESH HERB OIL & VINEGARS
They make wonderful gifts!

FLAVORED OIL

1 quart jar bottle and cork
Olive oil
1 lg. rosemary sprig
2 to 3 cloves garlic
2 red or green peppers
Garlic flowers

FLAVORED VINEGAR

1 quart jar bottle and cork
10 thin chives
Small basil sprigs
Rice vinegar
Raffia bow

Options:
Baby carrots
Corn
Red chili peppers
Peppercorns mixed colors
Basil
Italian parsley
Rosemary
Dill
Garlic cloves
Balsamic vinegar
Apple cider vinegar
Edible flowers

Put the cork inside the bottle. Notice where the bottom of the cork is. You will want to fill the bottle to just below that point.

Insert herbs, flowers and vegetables into bottle. Add oil or vinegar.

Firmly place cork in bottle. Tie a bow around the bottle.

Make a homemade tag by cutting paper into a rectangle. Fold in half and punch a hole in one corner. Write contents on front of tag and to/from info on the inside. Poke your ribbon through the hole and tie around the neck of the bottle.

It's also fun to use a wax stamp set to stamp your own insignia on the bottle. Place a few pretty herbs or flowers and a ribbon on the face of the bottle. Pour enough wax on them to attach them to the bottle, then seal it with your stamp.

You can also decorate the bottles with buttons and bows. Use a hot glue gun and your imagination!

Tips

How to get that garlic smell off your fingers

Place your fingers on a stainless steel knife or spoon and run it under cool water for about 10 seconds. The reaction between the stainless steel and the water molecules removes the odor.

Salt substitute

A slice of lemon squeezed over the cooked chicken adds a nice, tangy flavor.
It's also good over steamed veggies.

Buy fresh berries in the summer

They're cheaper when they're in season. Wash, clean, wrap and freeze them to use later in the year. Also try making a berry puree. Freeze in small containers to use instead of syrup.

Oil substitute

Use apple sauce instead of oil to bake desserts the low-fat way.
It's good in most quick breads, brownies and cakes.
(Not as moist as oil, but healthier for you.)

Ripening avocados

Toss the avocados in a paper bag and lay them in a shady spot
(like on top of the refrigerator) overnight. Really green avocados make take longer.
Note: Placing them in the sun will turn them brown. Don't ask me how I know.

Keep fruit salad from turning brown

Squeeze a little juice from lemon, lime, orange or pineapple over the fruit.
Note: If you use too much, it will change the taste of the fruit.

Fresh celery and carrot sticks

Stay fresher longer in a container of cold water, in the fridge.
I keep my nail polish in the fridge, too! Not packed in water though.

Chop onions without tears

Store your onions in the refrigerator. Rinse them in cold water before cutting.

Storing different types of fruit

Some types of fruit release gases which may cause others to spoil faster than usual. Store citrus separate from other types of fruit and vegetables. Potatoes should not be stored near apples. Bananas are best stored by themselves, since they bruise easily.

Carpet freshener

Baking soda is a great carpet freshener.
Sprinkle it on the floor. Wait 5 minutes, then vacuum up. Add a holiday scent to your house by sprinkling cinnamon and cloves on the carpet. Vacuum as usual.

Vinegar relief

Always keep some apple cider vinegar in the house. It's great for:

Getting out stains - Mix 1 part vinegar to 3 parts water. Dab into stain. Blot with a dry towel. Works well on pet stains if you get them early enough.

Getting odors off hands - Pour a little vinegar over your hands, then wash normally.

Helping to protect against bacteria - 1 part apple cider vinegar to 4 parts water. Drink it. It helps to cleanse the system. I take it if I feel like I'm coming down with something. It helps to prevent salmonella poisoning too.

Helping to prevent salmonella poisoning - Rinse your chicken in half vinegar and half water mixture. Let it sit for a minute or two in another dish. (Never re-use the same dish or package the chicken came in). Rinse with plain water. Cook normally.

Lemon degreaser

To remove grease and food odors from your hands, squeeze fresh lemon over them then wash your hands normally.

Fresh Drains

Pour baking soda in sink and tub drains to freshen them up.
Let it sit a couple of hours or overnight before rinsing.

A Clean Kitchen is a Healthy Kitchen

These days, we need to protect ourselves from harmful bacteria in our food. Here are some tips:

Wash utensils thoroughly - I wash my knives and mixing spoons between each thing I'm making or chopping.

Keep your cutting board clean - They say that plastic cutting boards are best. I have a wood one, but I clean it with diluted hydrogen peroxide or vinegar. I also don't cut much meat on it, since I usually go Pre-Fab. If I do cut meat on it, I either do it last or use a different cutting board for my veggies. After cleaning the cutting board, I let it dry thoroughly before using it again. Even when cutting veggies, I wash the cutting board between each variety. Yes, it may be overdoing it a bit, but I haven't gotten sick in...*well you don't really care how old I am, do you?*

Hydrogen peroxide

Keep it handy in the kitchen and bathroom.

Great kitchen disinfectant! Use a cleaning solution of 1 part hydrogen peroxide to 6 parts water. Use it to disinfect cutting boards, counter tops, dishwater, etc.

Clean your toothbrush - Pour hydrogen peroxide on your toothbrush. Rinse with hot water.

Smoking ovens

Pour salt or baking soda over messy oven spills to help stop the smoke. It also breaks down the burnt stuff to make cleaning up easier. When the oven is cool, scrape the spill off with a spatula.

Disposal

After squeezing lemons on your favorite dishes, toss the lemons into the disposal and run with water. The lemon rind helps to remove grime and leaves a nice scent.
You can pour your old boxes of baking soda down the drain to freshen it up, too.

Kitchen fires

Salt is a great kitchen helper! Throw it on a fire in a frying pan and put a lid on it. Use it on oven fires to put them out. Baking soda works too. In fact, if you have an electric stove baking soda seems to work better on a fire. **Never** throw water on a grease fire.
It spreads the flames and could splatter on you.

It's a good idea to keep a fire extinguisher near the kitchen, too.
Note: Be sure to get the correct type for a grease fire.
Also, check the expiration date on your fire extinguisher once a year.

Keep your hair away from the flames. Hair spray, nail polish and some types of makeup are flammable. So are scrunchies. I used to have the prettiest pink one.
Thank God it was a big sucker, I got it off just in time.

Use ice for discomfort

A little ice water can help to wash excess stomach acid from the esophagus, thus relieving the burning sensation in your throat. Don't drink too much, though, or it will hamper digestion.
Ice is also a great relief for muscle strains and bruises, headaches and neck pain.
A bag of frozen peas isn't bad, though. Neither is a cocktail.

Headaches

Avoid bananas, walnuts, chocolate, sweets and caffeine if possible, if you suffer from headaches.
These may have contributed to your headache in the first place and may intensify the pain. Try some fresh fruit (not bananas) and drink lots of water. Some say that drinking regular iced tea (not coffee) can help to relieve the pain from a headache. A massage is nice too!

There is also a pressure point at the top of both forearms (just below the elbow), that is very sensitive. If you feel around on your arm and find a point that hurts when you press on it, you've probably found it. Pressing gently on these acupressure points for about 16 seconds at a time may help to relieve the pain from your headache. At the very least, it will divert your attention from the pain in your head to the new pain in your arms.

When nothing else works, I turn off all the lights and noise, then lie down and close my eyes with a cold compress over my eyes and forehead. Relax and take a nap.
The world will wait for you. If your headache persists, see your doctor.

Food Combining for Better Digestion

Eating certain foods together can make it easier, *or more difficult* on your digestive tract.

Vegetables with carbohydrate (pasta, rice, potatoes, etc.) is good
Meat with vegetables is good
Fruit is best eaten by itself
Meat & starch = gas
Melons are best when eaten by themselves
Chocolate goes with anything. (Just kidding)
Pineapple after a meal will help with digestion
Papaya is good for digestion too, although not everyone likes it.
Peppermint tea also helps digestion. (It's really good with a ½ tsp. of honey)

Why does proper digestion matter? Well, besides the obvious, unless food is properly digested it can't be assimilated and used up by the body. Instead it's elements are stored in unsightly fat cells or scooted out of the body entirely. Some food combinations can even cause tummy rumbling and excess stomach acid. They also cause one to emit embarrassingly unfeminine sounds and foul odors. *(Farting)*

If your internal organs are making unladylike noises and causing discomfort
as a routine after meals, see your doctor - you may have a food allergy.

Eating tip for better digestion

Don't eat when you're upset. Stress can interfere with your natural digestive process causing "heartburn" or gas. Either way, it isn't pretty!

What's a doll to do? Starve? No, hon. Calm down first. Take a few deep breaths.
Concentrate on your breathing. Then eat.

You can think about killing that bum later.
Imagine his head exploding like a fiery balloon, bouncing back like rubber 'til his eyes bug out, then pop back in his head. *Ooh! That must have hurt. Heh heh.*
Watch it puffing up with the hot air you've known all along fills his head, until he's so big you think he's going to pop again...*can't wait, can you?* Then see him floating far, far away ~ way up in the sky ~ away from you ~ forgive, forget and release it.

Now, feel like having dessert?

SPILLS & STAINS

There are many great stain removers on the market. Here are a few home remedies:

Club soda is good for getting out many stains

Wine, soy sauce to name two. Dab it on as soon as possible with a clean cloth underneath. Press, but never rub a stain.

Vinegar

Gets out many types of stains. Use sparingly and blot it out.
Try a mild solution of vinegar and water on lace tablecloths.

Spilled eggs

Sponge up with cold water. It's not a good idea to re-use them.

Getting lipstick off your collar

Ha! You think I'm going to tell you?

Blood

Sprinkle talcum powder on stain to dry, then brush away. Soak fabric in cold water.
Pour detergent on stain and gently scrub sides of fabric together. Rinse in cold water.
Don't use hot water, it will set the stain.

To bleach a blood stain, pour hydrogen peroxide over it. Let it work for a minute, then wash fabric. *Note: Make sure your fabric is bleachable before using hydrogen peroxide.*

Chewing gum

Put ice on it. When it freezes, chip it off.

To get gum out of hair, smother it in peanut butter or baby oil.
Rub it out of the hair with your fingers. Have patience! It really works.

NATURAL PEST REPELLENTS

Most bugs don't like vitamin B

Taking B vitamins is a great way to ward off mosquitos, gnats and fleas. They seem to find the vitamin odor offensive. *Note: Those bugs seem to be most attracted to people who eat a lot of sweets. Apparently, they don't find chocolate offensive. But, who does?*

If you get stung anyway, put some meat tenderizer or papaya on it. The papain enzyme helps to break down poison and heal the sting. A baking soda salve also helps to absorb some of the venom. If you're roughing it, a dollop of cool mud will do the trick!

Protect your pets, too

Give them pet-style brewer's yeast tablets for natural flea control. Give them garlic for worms.

Bee stings

Cool mud will relieve the sting from bees. As it dries, it absorbs the venom. Vitamin C helps the body heal faster from a sting. If you are allergic to bees, seek medical attention immediately.

Ant Trails

Pour baby powder as a barrier. The ants won't walk across the powder because it clings to their skin and dries them out. A chalk line around your dog's dish should keep them out of his food, too. Diatomaceous earth is the best barrier. Ask about it at your local nursery.

Ants also don't like coffee grounds (but the plants and flowers love them!). Throw your used grounds into the garden and around the base of your house, to keep the ants out. Watch your garden flourish! *Note: Ants don't like boiling water poured on them either.*

Cedar

Keep moths out of your closet with cedar. Most drugstores have cedar blocks or balls you can hang in your closet or place in your dresser drawers.

Vinegar and water

Spray a mixture of equal parts of vinegar and water on sinks and counter tops to keep ants away. It also kills some of the harmful bacteria that grows on kitchen and bathroom surfaces.

HOW TO *STRETCH* YOUR MEAL

They're on their way and bringing eight more for dinner!

Last minute company? No problem!

HOW TO STRETCH YOUR MEAL

Meal type

TURKEY -

Nobody cares about seeing a whole bird on a plate anyway. Cut it up this year.   Rush to the Deli counter. Pick up a hunk of unsliced real turkey. Pull it apart with a fork, throw it in a pan with a little watered-down gravy. Heat it up and add it to your platter.

They're out of turkey?   Eh, chicken looks almost the same. Get a cooked one.

PASTA -

Pasta goes with almost anything! Cook some up and throw it in whatever else you're making.

RICE -

Same as pasta. Use one of those packaged types and serve it with whatever you're cooking.

MEAT -

Not enough meat for everyone? Chop it up and throw it in a large pot or soup kettle. Add chopped celery, onion, carrots, bouillon cubes and water. Stir a little cornstarch and cold water together, then add it to the stew to thicken it. Chop up some potatoes if you have them and throw them in the pot. Bring to boil and cook for 20 minutes. Lower heat and simmer until it's time to eat.

Drop in some dumplings if you dare. Dumpling dough - flour, water, chopped parsley, seasoning. Mix and form into lumps. Drop in stew or broth.

SNACKS -

Let them fill up on chips and dip. They'll have less room for dinner.

COOK SOMETHING ELSE -

Make a completely different dish from anything you've got in the fridge or pantry. Use the leftovers from last night's dinner. Serve a little of each dish to everyone at the table. Don't explain. They'll just think you couldn't make up your mind about what to serve.

DON'T WORRY ABOUT IT -

When all else fails, order in. Have a good time, enjoy your company, your family and friends. They are the reason you are getting together anyway. Remember, if the dinner is really bad, it will be a great conversation piece for your next party. The worse it is today, the funnier it will be tomorrow.

THE DAY AFTER

THE DAY AFTER
What to do with those leftovers

LEFTOVER TURKEY
Great Turkey Sandwich - Smear mayonnaise on two slices of bread. Smother them with turkey. Add cheese if you'd like. Place under broiler until mayonnaise begins to bubble (or cheese melts). Put both slices together. Indulge!

LEFTOVER FRUIT SALAD
Tropical Freeze - Throw your leftover fruit salad in a blender. Add rum & whirl.

LEFTOVER CRANBERRY SAUCE
Cranberry Twist - Drop it in a blender. Add ice and rum.

Hi-Pro Smoothie - Toss it the blender, add protein powder, nonfat frozen yogurt, ¼ cup. of fruit juice (apple or boysenberry) and crushed ice. Blend on high.

LEFTOVER PIZZA
Easy appetizers - Heat it up, slice into squares and follow with a Tropical Freeze.

LEFTOVER SALAD TOPPINGS
Snazz up any dish - Great in omelets, pasta, goulash. (No lettuce.)

LEFTOVER FLOWERS
Make Potpourri - Cut blossom heads off stems. Place blossoms on a cookie sheet in a single layer. Place in oven with pilot light. Do not turn oven on! Use a wad of aluminum foil to keep the oven door open a crack. Let the flowers dry overnight. Arrange potpourri in a bowl.

Options - Add sliced apples, oranges, whole cloves, allspice and cinnamon sticks. Sprinkle with extra cinnamon before drying. Add a few small pine cones to your potpourri for a wintery effect.

HOW TO GET OVER THAT FAT, DUMPY, LARD--FILLED, DEPRESSED FEELING WE GET FROM EATING NACHOS AND HOT FUDGE SUNDAES THE NIGHT BEFORE

No Guilt Allowed!

If you're going to indulge yourself, enjoy it fully. Each day is special, unique.
You really can make up for it the day after.

I get myself into trouble diet-wise when I "deprive" myself. If I'm feeling restricted, I want more. When I'm told I can't do something, it becomes the thing I want to do the most. So, when I wanted to lose weight, I stopped dieting and started concentrating on how foods made me feel after I ate them. I learned about their health content, what vitamins they had in them and tried to stay away from eating "empty calories". "Empty calories" is a name we've given to foods with very little nutritional value. You know, all the good stuff. Chocolate, sugar, cream puffs, potato chips, etc.

I started concentrating on me. I tossed out the bathroom scale and all my calorie-counters. I began to focus on what made me happy, gave me comfort. What was it about food that I enjoyed the most? Why was food so important to me? Was it a replacement for something missing in my life?

Well, at first I got really depressed. I had dreams I was running down the frozen food isle of the grocery store, stuffing my face with chocolate eclairs. Show's you how deprived I felt, normally I would have let them thaw before eating 'em.

Finally, I went to the health food store and read books about nutrition and healthful food combinations. I was amazed at how simple it was. Now, I don't limit myself, I limit the "funk food", foods that make me feel in a "funk" after I eat them. I try to stay away from sugar, butter, high fat dairy products and red meat.

I've found that although a quart of ice cream tastes fabulous going down, a parfait glass of fresh strawberries makes me feel better afterwards. Indulging in foods without a lot of fat and sugar gives me pep, makes me feel sexier, and gets rid of my zits - yes, doll, even at my age.

Of course, there are those days when nothin' but nachos will do it for me. I will then treat myself with the full knowledge of how I'll look, feel and fit into my jeans the day after...and I'll enjoy it none the less.

That's the secret. When you enjoy each day, do things that you want to do, eat what you want to eat, you don't want as much, because you have it all. You don't need to fill voids in your life, because there aren't any. If you decide you want to change something about yourself, do it for you. For how a healthful lifestyle will make you feel both physically and mentally.

Add nutritious foods to your meals. I try to throw extra veggies into everything. Pile them on! I get so full and satisfied over the blend of flavors and amount of food, that most of the time, I don't even want dessert. Well, unless my husband asks me...you know how they get that look in their eyes, kinda sway their heads back and forth, and say in that really, low, smooth voice..."how about some dessert, baby?" The first time you see it, you laugh your head off. But, afterwards, you're glad that you didn't eat so much you have to unzip your pants and lay down in the back of the station wagon on the way home from the restaurant.

Remember, you're in control. When you don't feel guilty and don't deprive yourself, you don't want as much anyway. *And if anybody picks on you, punch 'em.*

Anyway, here are a few of my tricks for "cleaning out" the day after:

LEMON & WATER -

Squeeze a half a lemon into a glass of water. It cuts the mucus in your throat. Some say it helps to cleanse the liver, too.

TAKE A WALK IN THE GARDEN - Great for cleansing the mind.

Look at the birds and flowers. Don't think, just observe.

They say bluebirds bring happiness. Don't stand under one for too long, though, or they'll give you a little more than you wanted.

A SMELLY BREW -

A clove of garlic (chopped), a tablespoon of fresh chopped parsley, two tablespoons of apple cider vinegar in 8 oz. of water. It helps to cleanse the system and ward off cold and flu bugs. If you drink too much of it, it will ward your friends off, too.

TAKE A BATH -

Or a shower. Scrub your skin gently with a loofah to remove dead skin cells. Wash your hair, shave your legs, give yourself a facial.

EXERCISE -

I know, everybody says to exercise. It really does make you feel good. Start slow, a little at a time. Be gentle with yourself ~ and *Breathe*! Taking deep, relaxed breaths when exercising can help to release some toxins in your system. If you use weights, breathe out on the hard stuff, in on the release. Then, stretch afterwards.

VITAMINS & HERBS -

There are many good vitamin supplements and herbal remedies on the market these days. Consult with your doctor or chiropractor on which health supplements are the best for you. I take *"ULTIMATE CLEANSE"* and *"REZYME" by NATURE'S SECRET* when I want to "clean out." *"ULTIMATE CLEANSE"* is a wonderful blend of herb and fiber tablets that work very well in detoxifying my system. *"REZYME"*, is a nutritional supplement which helps to digest food while nourishing the digestive tract (so I don't get gas). Both of these were formulated by *Dr. Lindsey Duncan, C.N., N.D.* He has other fabulous products from *NATURE'S SECRET* that are also great for the bod.

I can't stress enough the importance of consulting with a health expert before starting a new nutritional program. Bodies are different and have varying needs. What is good for me may not be the right thing for you. So, find out just what is right for your body and if you are allergic to anything, from an expert.

Also remember, when taking vitamins, more is not necessarily better. Too much can even be harmful in some cases. Our bodies tend to store up an excess of certain vitamins until they're needed. If we keep taking them, our storage areas never get used up. Sometimes taking too much of one vitamin can cause the body to deplete itself of others. For example, when you lose a lot of water, such as when you sweat or take too many water soluble vitamins (C, B) you may lose too much potassium. Potassium is vital to a properly functioning body. Depletion of it may cause dizziness, nausea and disorientation. Too much isn't good either.

Don't be afraid, though. Consult with your chiropractor or doctor, read some books on health, nutrition and alternative remedies. You can take control of your health and your life. It's really easier than you may think. I've found, it's best to do things in moderation...and to follow directions.

EAT A GREAT BREAKFAST - A great breakfast is one that gives you the energy you need to start your day. Fruit is wonderful for breakfast. Smoothies with protein powder are fabulous! Bran muffins are great! Nuke one for about minute and eat it plain! Add jelly made without sugar if you want, skip the butter. Take your vitamins and go.

LUNCH - Go out for a huge salad. Dip your bread in the salad dressing instead of using butter. (Do it when no one is looking.) Or, try eating bread without butter. Good bread tastes better that way anyway. Drink water with lemon.

DINNER - By this time, you should be feeling much better. Our bodies have a wonderful way of cleaning out our toxins if we treat them right. Now it's up to you. If you skip the funk foods tonight, you'll feel better in the morning. You can always be decadent another day! *Or in another way*.

FOR
THE
BOD

FOR THE BOD
Ready-to-wear foods

BANANA

Wet hair. Mash banana and spread on ends of hair. Leave on for 15 minutes,
then wash hair.   It makes a great pre-conditioner for softer hair!

MAYONNAISE

Softens dry hair! Rub about 2 Tbsp. mayonnaise into the hair. Leave on for about 15 minutes.
Then, shampoo as you normally do.

AVOCADO

Facial mask, moisturizing. The vitamin A in the avocado is good for the skin,
too. Leave on for 5 minutes. Scrape off with tortilla chips (just kidding). Wash off.

EGG WHITE

Facial mask, toner. Beat egg white gently, spread on face in upward strokes.
Leave on for about 20 minutes. It will tighten up. Whatever you do,
don't answer the door!

HONEY

Heat honey slightly (not too hot), pat onto face. Diminishes blackheads.
Option: Add a small amount of honey to beaten egg whites.
Give it a few good stirs, then pat on face. Leave on for about 20 minutes.
Wash with a good facial cleanser while **gently** scrubbing with a loofah.
Note: *This mixture will remain sticky. Don't lay your face on anything
you'd rather not carry with you while you're wearing it.*

PLAIN YOGURT

Apply to face. Semi-moisturizing. Acidophilus cultures are good for the skin.

PAPAYA

Apply mashed papaya to face. It softens and removes dead skin cells.
Make sure papaya isn't too ripe though. Fermented papaya may make your skin red.
Test a little on your forearm first. Wash off with loofa sponge and a mild facial cleanser.

CUCUMBER

Place cucumber slices on your eyelids to reduce puffiness and brighten the eyes. (It will cause your eyes to water a little bit. Remove your makeup first). Lay on your bed and elevate your feet (on pillows or against the wall). Relax for 15 minutes then wash your face, finishing with cold water.

LEMON

One half of a lemon, squeezed into a large glass of water is a fabulous
cleansing drink. They say it's good for the liver.
It's also good on the elbows ~ to remove the dead flaky skin. Not the sags though.
If you know of a remedy for sagging skin, let me know.

DISTILLED WATER & ALOE VERA SPRITZ

Fill a mist bottle with filtered or distilled water. Add 3 Tbsp. pure aloe vera gel.
Shake. Mist face during the day. It freshens ~ even over make-up.

TEA BAGS

Reduces puffiness around the eyes. Steep them for a minute, then press the water out.
When cooled, place them on the eyelids. Relax for 10 minutes.

BEAUTIFUL BATHING

There are many wonderful bath products on the market. Use them to add fun and fragrance to your baths and showers. Some products can make you feel better too!

Aromatic Oils

Pour a few drops of aromatic oil into your bath water as the tub begins to fill. There are many types of oils with delicious fragrances to make you feel marvelous! Many health food and specialty stores carry aromatic oils. Read the descriptions and choose the oils best for you.

Bubble bath

These days, there are so many types to choose from you'll be able to find the perfect bubbles for your every mood.

Baking soda

Add a few tablespoons of baking soda to your bath. It pulls some of the toxins from your skin.

Candles

Place candles in safe places, away from your hair and other flammable things, and light them. Play soft music and turn the lights down. Add bubbles to your bath and soak your stress away.

Tea

You can add a few herbal tea bags to your bath instead of aromatic oils. Camomile for relieving tension. Peppermint or spearmint to perk you up. Comfrey to help minor aches and bruises feel better. If you make your bath water too strong, you might want to shower afterwards to get the tea off. Don't drink the water...

Mineral Salts

If you're feeling a bit depleted or have minor aches and pains, a mineral bath might be the perfect thing to perk you up. These days, even the grocery stores are carrying them. Look for bath therapies or bath salts at a store near you. Don't soak too long ~ prune fingers aren't pretty.

Bathing buddies

These are always fun to have in the bath.

FANTASY DINNERS
Let Him Cook For You!

Pick out the flyers from your favorite restaurants that deliver. Let *him* choose the meals and order. Get back in the jacuzzi until your food arrives.

Or ~

Let him barbecue clams and shellfish.
Dip them in garlic butter melting in an all metal pan on the grill.
Sip your favorite beverage while you cuddle and watch the sunset.

FOR DAD

There are other ways to cook besides the barbecue

Our Dad was the inspiration for this book.

Recently divorced after 30 years of marriage -- So, it was to three wives, who's counting? He's now out on his own, again.

For a very special dinner, he decided to cook lobster tails. He got his butter out, melted it perfectly, placed the lobster tails in the oven, set it on broil -- then went upstairs to take a shower!

Several minutes pass. Smoke begins to fill the kitchen. Hmm! He's thinking...
something smells awfully good. The neighbors must be barbecuing.

Fire alarms go off. Oh, no! The patter of little wet feet are heard, running to the kitchen. The oven door swings open - then, Clang! Thud. Aou! Aou! Aou!

Needless to say. He went out for dinner that evening.

We bought him a new pan and an oven mitt for Christmas.

Hey, DAD! Here's a section just for you!

HOW TO BOIL WATER

Fill a pot with cold water and place it on the stove. Turn the burner under the pot on high. The water will start to bubble. Let it boil for at least 1 minute (3-5 min. is better). This will get rid of off any bacteria or chemical residue in the water. Then, reduce heat and add whatever else you're going to make.

If you ever have to boil drinking water after a flood or something, boil it longer ~ like 10 to 15 minutes. Then, strain it through a cotton shirt or cheesecloth to get rid of the dirt and stuff.

Tip from Flo: If you have a gas stove, make sure the burner is lit. If it won't light, check the pilot. Wait for any gas to dissipate before re-lighting the pilot. You don't need to lean over and watch it light closely. Keep your head away from the stove, just in case.

HOW TO MAKE TEA OR COCOA IN THE MICROWAVE

Fill a cup with water. Nuke on high for 1 minute. Remove from oven. Add tea bag or cocoa mix (*and marshmallows*).

HOW TO MAKE TEA OR COCOA WITHOUT A MICROWAVE

Look for the tea kettle. It may be on the stove or in a cupboard. Fill it with water. Turn the stove on to the highest setting. Place the tea kettle on the stove. It will either whistle or blow steam out of its spout when the water is hot. Fill a cup with the hot water and add flavorings.

CORN ON THE COB

Peel and discard the husk and stringy things. Wrap the cob in two paper towels, making sure the entire ear of corn is covered. Run it under the faucet to get it wet. Place it in the microwave and nuke on high for about 11 minutes.

Serve with those cute little corn holders. Use butter or yogurt for a flavoring, if you need it.

Dad's favorite corn flavoring: Roll corn in plain yogurt and Parmesan cheese. Mmm!

BAKED POTATOES

Gently scrub and rinse the potatoes.   Wrap each potato in paper towels, covering them entirely. Get the paper towels a little wet, but not soaked.

Place the potatoes in the microwave (*no more than two at a time)* and nuke on high for about 5 minutes. After 5 minutes, turn them and cook them for 5 more minutes. Let stand 3 minutes.

Use a potholder to remove them from the oven. Squeeze each one gently to check if they're done. They should give just a little and be soft in the middle. Wrap in towel or potholder to keep warm until you serve.

For fluffy potatoes, microwave them until they're almost done, then pop them in a pre-heated oven (set at 425) for about 10 minutes. The skin should be crispy and the insides should be fluffy.

Optional garnishes:
> **Butter or margarine**
> **Parmesan cheese**
> **Sour cream**
> **Yogurt**
> **Chives**
> **Chopped onions**
> **Cheese**
> **Broccoli**

TWICE BAKED POTATOES

Milk
Butter
Seasoning
Green onion (diced)
Cheddar cheese (grated)

Cook the potatoes as suggested in the recipe on the previous page. Cut a long slit in each potato and spoon the insides into a bowl.

Add a little milk, butter, seasoning, chopped green onion or chives and mash it up.

Spoon the mixture back into the potato skins and top with cheese. Place them on a microwaveable dish and nuke for a minute or two, until the cheese melts. Garnish immediately with a little chopped green onion or chives.

Low-cal version - Substitute water or chicken broth for milk and non-fat yogurt for butter. Add fresh spinach, diced red onion and seasoning. Omit the cheese.

CINDY'S BBQ CHICKEN

¾ cup orange juice
6 Tbsp. honey
6 Tbsp. mustard
2 tsp. fresh chopped rosemary
Boneless skinless chicken meat

Marinate overnight in the fridge. Barbecue to perfection the next day! Incredibly delicious!

FROZEN ENTREES

Frozen entree (your favorite)
Frozen side dishes (vegetables)
2 quarts water
Garnish

*Hide the packages and no one will know
you didn't make this meal from scratch!
(Unless they have the recipe too!)*

Fill a sauce pan with water and bring
to boil.

With a knife, carefully slit the end of
the box containing the pouches of
frozen side dishes. DO NOT
PIERCE THE POUCHES.

Slowly slide the pouches into the
boiling water. The water will
automatically cool to a simmer.
When it returns to a boil, lower the
heat and simmer for 5-10 minutes.

While that's cooking, open the box
containing the frozen entree. Slit a
small hole in the plastic wrap and
pop that baby in the microwave.
Read the package for heat level and
cooking duration.

When your side dishes are cooked,
remove the plastic pouches from the
hot water with a fork or tongs. Place
them on a flat surface (a plate will do
nicely). Slit the pouch on the side
that is away from you (unless of
course, you'd like to steam your
face). Then, up end it and let the
contents slide onto your plate or
serving platter.

Repeat the process until all the side
dish pouches are empty.

Remove the entree from the
microwave and arrange the contents
on your plate or platter. Garnish.
with parsley or twisted orange.

DINNER FOR TWO

2 artichokes
Steamed vegetables
Filets of fish
Pumpernickel rolls

Fill the large bottom pan with 3" of water. Place the colander inside pot.

Wash the artichokes and cut off their stems at the base of the leaves. Place them inside the colander. *(For an added flair you can snip off the sharp point of each leaf with scissors.)* Place the lid on the top of the pot.

Turn the stove on medium high. The water will start to boil. Check the water level in 15 minutes.

The artichokes are done when their leaves can be pulled off easily. Cook approximately 45 minutes. They are overdone when they fall apart (but they are very good that way.)

While that's cooking - Get out the vegetables you picked up today from the salad bar.

Broccoli tops (they look like little
  green bouquets)
½ cup onion (diced)
Zucchini (sliced)
Yellow squash
  (sliced like the zucchini)
Green bell pepper
  (chop the strips in half)
Red bell pepper
  (chop the strips in half)

Place these vegetables inside the smaller colander.

Add 2 fillets of your favorite *FISH.* Lay the fish on top of the vegetables. Squeeze a lemon over the fish.

Sprinkle with your favorite seasoning or fresh dill.

Optional Tasty Seasoning: Sprinkle a little garlic and Parmesan cheese over the food while cooking.

Take the lid off the pot you are cooking your artichokes in. Add the smaller colander (which is filled with rest of your dinner) to this pot. Keep the artichokes cooking. Check the water level. If necessary, add more water, but don't add so much water that it covers the artichokes. If you keep the water level just below the base of the artichokes, you'll save more vitamins.

However, if you don't have a steamer for them to rest in, don't worry about it. Just let them bob around in the water. You can take vitamins later.

Now, place the lid back on the pot. You have about 15 minutes until dinner is ready. You can mix a drink, take a *quick* shower, or arrange a nice bouquet of flowers for the table.

Check to see if the fish is done. It should be flaky when you tap it with a fork. The vegetables should be soft and colorful. An artichoke leaf should pull off easily. If the artichokes still aren't done, let them cook a little longer while you melt the butter or put the mayonnaise in a dish for dipping.

Serve dinner with pumpernickel rolls for an added zip.

BARBECUED VEGGIES

Yellow & green zucchini
Mushrooms
Bell peppers (red, green and yellow)
Pearl onions (peeled or canned & drained)
Olive oil
Garlic
Herbs (rosemary or Italian blend or
      favorite seasoning)

Chop vegetables into chunks and place on foil. Sprinkle a little oil on top. Add garlic and seasoning. Wrap up tightly and cook on the barbecue. Turn frequently to avoid burning.

OR -

Bake in oven for 10 minutes.

SHRIMP KABOBS

Shrimp
Pineapple chunks
Onion chunks
Bell pepper chunks
Low-salt soy sauce
Lemon juice
3 Tbsp. grated ginger
¼ cup honey

Option: Substitute steak or chicken for shrimp

Alternate the shrimp, pineapple, onion and bell pepper on skewers. Lay in some type of pan.

Cover in soy sauce, juice from one lemon, ginger and honey. Marinate for 30 minutes in the fridge.

Barbecue until shrimp is done (turns pink). Serve over cooked rice.

BARBECUED CLAMS

Live little-neck clams
½ cup butter
2 Tbsp. garlic
2 cups clam juice
1 tsp. lemon juice
Crusty bread

Place butter, garlic, lemon and clam juices in metal pan. (*Make sure the handle is metal too. Keep an oven mitt handy.*)

Melt mixture at back of barbecue grill.

Cook clams on grill until they open. Skewer the meat with a long toothpick or wooden skewer. Dip in butter mixture. Eat. Cook more clams.

Take a piece of crusty bread and *oh no!* You dropped it in the butter mixture! Well, don't let it go to waste. Mmm!

TERIYAKI TUNA

Fresh Ahi tuna
1 onion (sliced)
1 red bell pepper (sliced)
1 green bell pepper (sliced)
Mushrooms (sliced)
Lemon
Teriyaki sauce
Fresh ginger

Option: Roll tuna steaks in coarsely ground pepper and sear over fire for a few minutes. They should be slightly uncooked inside. Slice into thin pieces and serve over salad.

Cut tuna into steaks. Slice vegetables. Place tuna steaks and vegetables in a dish. Pour teriyaki sauce and squeeze lemon over top. Grate fresh ginger and place all around.

Cover and refrigerate for about 15 minutes. Barbecue tuna until done. Cook vegetables in foil or a pan on the grill. Serve together.

BEACH BAKE
Cook at the beach while you play in the surf. Bake your bod and dinner at the same time!

Dig -

Find a good spot on the beach where it's legal to have a fire.

Dig a hole in the sand 3 to 4 feet deep.

Line it with oak or other hardwood.

Lay rocks around the wood.

Light a big fire and let it burn for 3 to 4 hours, while you sunbathe and swim.

Bake -

After the fire subsides, the rocks will still be very hot.

Lay seaweed on the rocks and cover it with gauze.

Wrap your food securely in aluminum foil ~ unless you like the taste of sand in your food.

Lay your food in a towel on the seaweed.

Drip a little seawater on the towel to create steam.

Cover it with sand or a heavy tarp and let it bake for about an hour.

About fifteen minutes before you eat, toss a wrapped loaf of crusty bread in to warm it up.

Good foods to cook this way are:

Clams (they open and make everything taste better)

Seafood, shellfish

Chicken (pre-cooked)*

Corn on the cob

Potatoes

Vegetables braised with oil and garlic

*We pre-cook the chicken until it's almost done, at home, then beach bake it the rest of the way.

After about an hour, dig out your dinner ~ Remember, it may be hot.
'might be a good idea to use a mitt to unwrap it.

Snuggle under a blanket and nibble on your lobster while you gaze
at the setting sun on the horizon.

Life is fun, isn't it?

INDEX